DREAMS
How to have them

PLANS
How to make them

GOALS
How to reach them

DREAMS
How to have them

PLANS
How to make them

GOALS
How to reach them

Ken Gaub

New Leaf Press

First printing: July 1993
Eighth printing: December 2005

ISBN: 0-89221-244-6
Library of Congress Catalog Number: 93-86325

Printed in the United States of America

Please visit our website for other great titles:
www.newleafpress.net

For information regarding author interviews, please
contact the publicity department at (870) 438-5288.

Endorsements

The book is terrific; I will make it mandatory reading for my staff. It's straight forward, no extremes.
DALE CARPENTER, Senior Pastor, Stone Church, Yakima, WA

Ken Gaub writes from his heart and from his personal experience. He does the things he writes about — and he does them consistently and well. His dedication to his convictions is unquestioned.
RAY E. SMITH, General Superintendent, Open Bible Standard Churches, Des Moines, IA

When I read the manuscript, my heart filled with excitement as I thought of the people whose dreams would become realities after reading the book.
DAN WOLD, successful entrepreneur, Portland, OR

Ken Gaub is a man who thoroughly understands the importance of goals in life. Nothing will help a man surmount his difficulties, survive his circumstances, lift him and keep him healthy and enthusiastic more than purpose in life. Ken Gaub, in his unique way, will challenge you to strive to become all that God intends for you to be.
KENNY FOREMAN, Senior Pastor, Cathedral of Faith, San Jose, CA

Ken Gaub is a personal friend. I have traveled most of the world with him. He is unselfish, and a man of integrity. I recommend his writings to my readers. You will find both interest and instruction in what he has written.

C.M. WARD, retired Revivaltime radio speaker, Stockton, CA

Ken Gaub always arrests attention! When he speaks, I listen, and I'm not alone. His wise words will toughen the heart and teach powerful principles that put us in a place of real possibility.

RON HEMBREE, President, "Life's Lessons," author of over 40 books, TV & radio personality, Phoenix, AZ

Ken Gaub is a master motivator. In his down-to-earth, easy to understand, humorous style, he shows you how to tap your dreams, make plans to achieve your goals.

DAVE WILLIAMS, Senior Pastor, Mount Hope Church, author of several books, Lansing, MI

In this book, Ken Gaub shares that God-given dreams, backed with mountain-moving faith, translated into productive action, result in accomplished goals. This is motivational reading for everyone.

PAUL WALKER, Ph.D., Senior Pastor, Mount Paran Church of God, Atlanta, GA

Dedicated to:

- My parents, John and Millie Gaub, whose prayers, support, faith, encouragement, wisdom, and lives set an example for me.

- My grandchildren, Jannessa, Jourdan, Joshua, Austin, and Brittney, who gave me the inspiration for the part on monsters.

- My staff, board members, personal friends, and supporters, whose prayers, support, and encouragement is helping us touch a lot of lives in a hurting world.

Special thanks to:

Pastor Dave Williams for some great insights and help.

If you would like to write Ken Gaub
or have him speak to your church or group,
he can be contacted through:

YOUTH OUTREACH UNLIMITED
P.O. Box 1
Yakima, WA 98097
(509) 575-1965
FAX (509) 575-4732

Contents

Part II: Plans

Part III: Goals

Foreword

K en Gaub has a passion for eagles. I have seen him carry home wooden eagles, brass eagles, every kind under the sun from all over the world. For many years he lived and traveled in a Silver Eagle bus. I believe he loves eagles because they are such magnificent creatures with powerful telescopic vision. They can see their tiny prey from great altitudes and swoop down upon it with unerring accuracy.

Ken has eagle vision! He sees further than most. He has a gift to see what God can do in difficult situations. Linked with that is a compelling passion for all kinds of people. I have seen him "create an opportunity" to share words of encouragement with people wherever he found them. Whether a weary waitress in a truck stop cafe, an

Arab donkey driver on the deserts of Jordan, or a business executive in an airplane, Ken has a unique ability to see the possibilities in people, and he cares. It is not unusual to see his eyes flood with emotion when he talks about what God has done in a life that was hurting.

Ken is a most interesting person, because he has a curious mind. "Have you ever wondered?" is a favorite expression he uses often. He probes into areas that most people never think about. This son of a country preacher was raised in the simple setting of a rural parsonage where he learned from a godly father the principles of honesty, hard work, and loyalty, almost to a fault. When you add to that generosity, you have a most unusual man. It is not unusual for Ken on the spur of the moment to write out a check to make a payment on a van for a struggling evangelist when his own finances are at rock bottom.

This book is pure Ken Gaub. His message flows naturally and easily from the wellspring of his heart. God, in His love, sends such special people into our lives to extend our vision to the horizons of faith. Ken Gaub is such a man. We are special friends, and I'm his pastor.

— Dale Carpenter
Pastor, Stone Church, Yakima, WA
General Presbyter, Assemblies of God

Preface

Wouldn't it be wonderful if all your dreams came true; your plans were perfectly laid out and executed; and every goal you set was reached on the target date?

What if everything you wanted to do came to pass and all the things you hoped for happened: a successful career or maybe a dream home or a luxury automobile or a vacation somewhere in the world?

Perhaps your dreams are more altruistic: the ability to help the poor, full support for a ministry, or a missionary venture to some faraway land.

I trust that some of the thoughts in this book will encourage you with your own dreams . . . and plans . . . and goals.

— Ken Gaub

Part I

Dreams

1

Get Ready to Dream

God is the Giver of worthwhile dreams. God, who created mankind in His image, endowed us with a will of our own and gave us (among other things) the ability to dream.

God himself has a dream for mankind. It is His desire that His children live pure and holy lives that are whole and healthy and blessed in every way. He wants to commune with His children to bring us true peace and the desires of our heart.

> *God's dream is for His children to succeed in every way.*

The Bible says, "I wish above all things that you would prosper, and be healthy" (3 John 2).

Are You a Dreamer?

Most of us also would like to leave this world having made a positive mark on those around us. Dreamers are the people who accomplish the deeds that history remembers.

The size and scope of our dreams vary, however, as do our motives. Some dreams tend to be selfish; others are selfless. Most of us have both kinds of dreams.

Jesus admonished, "Seek first the kingdom of God, and His righteousness, and all these things shall be added unto you" (Matt. 6:33). If we seek God's will for our lives, our dreams will fall into their proper place.

We, however, have to plan and work to make our dreams happen. We cannot just say, "Whatever is to be will be." We must exert ourselves in an organized way in order to see our dreams come to pass.

Maybe you have a dream, but you're afraid to verbalize it or even pray about it because you're afraid it won't come to pass. If that's the case, let me ask you something: What grows on a lake that is frozen over in winter? Absolutely nothing!

The same thing can happen to your mind if you're not open to trying new ideas to advance your life.

> *Without dreams, plans, and goals, you place limits on what God can do for you.*

Placing Limits on God

How do we place limits on God and paralyze our ability to dream? Let's look at several things that can stop us from dreaming.

1. Feelings of worthlessness.

Sometimes people have a sense of self depreciation. I've heard some say, "I am not important; I'm no good; I don't have the right qualifications to do anything worthwhile."

We all feel like worthless nobodies at certain times in our life. It's when we start to *act* like worthless nobodies that our present and future suffer.

Some say, "I have a dream, but it won't really work for me. It's impossible. I'm whipped. I failed before, and I'll fail again. It won't happen. I don't know what to do," and on and on they go with negative thinking and talking.

> ***They totally paralyze their
> success and productivity by
> their talk of worthlessness.***

What they are actually saying is that God makes junk and doesn't know what He is doing.

2. Believing the worst.

Whenever the media states, "We are in a recession," people lose confidence, quit buying, and more people are thrown out of work. As a result the cycle widens, and soon there really is a recession.

Larry King, on the "Larry King Live" show, asked former president Richard Nixon, "What is a recession?"

Nixon answered, "A recession is any time people lose confidence in the future and think there are no answers."

Don't let brainwashing by the negative news media rob you of the positive that God can help you do.

3. Dwelling on your circumstances.

Do you constantly think about problems and challenges that you are probably *never* going to have to face?

People say, "My situation is hopeless."

> ***There is no such thing as a hopeless situation, but people can grow hopeless about situations.***

Your attitude is more important than your finances, your I.Q., or your circumstances. We can't deny circumstances, but we can refuse to dwell on them and allow them to paralyze our mind.

The down and out come from different backgrounds but so do successful people who have succeeded with their dreams — some were high school dropouts and others were born with silver spoons in their mouths.

What then makes the difference between who succeeds and who fails? The failures are beaten down by unfavorable circumstances, give up, and let life pass them by. But those who are successful overcome their circumstances, have dreams, and pursue those dreams.

You can use your mind to gain a measure of control over circumstances. If you feed into it things that will make you grow — the Bible, challenging biographies of successful people, and good teaching — growth will take place in your life. By contrast, if you feed on garbage and dwell on the negative side of life, you will be headed straight down the road to failure.

> *Depression begins in a*
> *paralyzed mind.*

4. Yielding to depression.

You can choose to be happy and content, or you can allow sadness and despair to rule your emotions. It's a matter of choice. Some people earn millions of dollars, but their lives are empty and dull, while others earn only a few thousand, yet their lives are full and exciting. You can also have money, be excited, and lead a happy successful life.

I realize that we all experience low periods in our life, but we do not have to allow them to paralyze our mind. You lose the balance in your life when you magnify your problems.

In the past, I've personally hit tough spots where I felt like giving up. But when I dealt with the situation and my feelings, I was able to overcome the problem.

Without a continued feeling of growth or something worthwhile, you can develop a chronic state of depression. When your mind becomes paralyzed, you become your own worst enemy. Be your own cheerleader. The Bible says that David encouraged himself in the Lord. Take action, be decisive, and choose to be a happy person.

Someone who has reached a point of depression where he/she can't seem to deal with things on his/her own, should seek professional help, either from a doctor or a qualified minister. Full blown, clinical depression is a serious condition, but it responds readily and quickly to proper medical treatment.

Freeing the Paralyzed Mind

So what's the best treatment for a mind paralyzed by poor self-worth, a negative attitude toward life, overwhelming circumstances, and depression?

The apostle Paul wrote to Timothy, "God has not given us the spirit of fear, but of power, and of love, and of a sound mind" (2 Tim. 1:7).

How can you free your paralyzed mind? Put these suggestions into action:

1. Believe you are a person of worth.

You can't believe in others unless you believe in yourself, and you can't really believe in yourself unless you believe in God. Do you know that you're an original, a choice creation, special, one of a kind? You are great because God made you to be great.

Some feel that it is prideful to feel good about yourself. How could it be wrong to love what God loves? Be good to yourself. Know that you are somebody.

If you take a twenty dollar bill and crumple it up, it is still worth twenty dollars. Even if you throw it on the ground and stomp on it, it is still valued at twenty dollars. Satan may knock you down and stomp on you, but you are still very valuable to God.

Remember, you are important to God. He forgives you, qualifies you, and gives you value. Satan can do nothing to alter that fact.

Don't let Satan bring accusations against you and turn your thoughts in the direction of defeat. You need to know the difference between being accused and convicted. Judas Iscariot and Simon Peter are good examples.

> *It's not mind over matter. If you don't mind, it won't matter!*

Judas allowed Satan to badger him into betraying Jesus. (See Luke 22:3-5.) He was later so sorry for what he had done that he committed suicide. Satan's accusation led to Judas' death.

Peter also failed Jesus, and was also sorry. (See Luke 22:55-62.) He was convicted of his sin. Conviction led him to repentance and a better future.

2. Start the day with a positive attitude.

In the morning, get out of bed, get dressed, and get your Bible. Start the day thinking about God. Don't allow the world to close in on you and mold you into their image.

Read some of the many promises in the Bible: "My peace I leave with you" (John 14:27). "Don't let your heart be troubled" (John 14:1). "My God shall supply all your need" (Phil. 4:19), and others too numerous to mention.

You will feel better because the Word of God is in your thoughts. You will get excited about the day. Say to yourself, "I'm going to have a great day!" Then start tackling the challenges.

A calm person with good thoughts knows how to adapt. As the day ends, you will look back on the problems and challenges that have been easily surmounted. Because the day has been rewarding, you will go to bed free of negative thoughts.

I saw a sign in Hong Kong that read, "Take every emergency leisurely."

Plant the soil of your mind full of good thoughts, and the crop you raise will be wholesome. In this stressful age, this is extremely important, but positive thinking alone will not give you the victory over defeat that you need. You've got to take another step.

> *All your problems will yield
> to solutions.*

3. Define your dreams.

God gives the birds food, but they have to fly to find it. You can't just sit and do nothing, expecting God to do it all.

That's where dreams, plans, and goals come in.

Most of the miracles in the Bible happened because someone acted upon a command from

God or from a prophet and did something. The widow borrowed jars to fill; another widow baked the prophet a cake; a blind man went to the pool and washed. There are many more examples. Get out your Bible concordance and look them up.

I don't think anyone ever made plans to live on Skid Row. But they allowed circumstances to beat them down. Some of them say they had bad luck. I don't believe in luck — bad, good, or otherwise. Luck of any kind won't get you where you want to go, but planning and working will.

Suppose a farmer wants milk. He realizes that he must get that milk from a cow. He doesn't sit on a stool out in the field waiting for the cow to back up to him so that he can milk her.

If you want success in any area of your life, you have to have a dream and plans to reach that dream.

Joan, a young French peasant girl, dreamed of setting France free from her enemies. Many thought she was crazy, but she somehow persuaded the heir apparent to the French throne that she had a dream and that her dream was from God. The then future king, Charles VII, put her in charge of all his armies, and she led the French army to victory in 1429. Her military strategy conquered the city of Orleans, and she went on to defeat the enemy in four more battles. Joan of Arc had a dream.

My good friend, Pastor Dave Williams, who has a wonderful ministry and a great church in Lansing, Michigan, said in one of his books, *Define*

Your Dreams: "You must know what your dreams are before you ever make plans for them. If you can't write down your God-given dreams on a sheet of paper, you are never going to make any plans whatsoever. Ask God to guide you, but be sure you know what the dream is and that your motives are pure."[1]

Your life moves in the direction of your most dominant thoughts. Remember what your dreams are. Write them down.

> *It's a lot easier to make plans when you know who you are, where you are, and where you are going.*

4. Know where you are going.

Before I go some place to speak, I know where I am starting my journey. When I call to reserve a seat on the necessary flights, the first thing the agent wants to know is my starting point. She cannot give me a route nor a price until she knows where I am.

I also know exactly where I am going. I don't go to the airport and get on just any airplane; I have it all set up in advance. It is written down on my calendar. The ticket is purchased to the city where I am speaking. I have made my plans, I follow through, so I arrive at my destination.

That's the way it is with dreams. Dreams aren't something we just lie around thinking about, hoping someday they'll come to pass. We have to start somewhere and have a final target in mind.

But whatever your dreams, always remember where you came from: Your real beginning is in God.

Joseph had a God-given dream that kept him going throughout very difficult circumstances. In spite of his brothers' ridicule and hatred, he pursued his dream. Even when sold into slavery, he saw himself as God saw him — as a person of great worth and value. In the dark prison chambers, Joseph never gave up. He didn't consider himself a prisoner, he knew who he was, where he had come from, and where he was going. He acted like a responsible person, took charge of his life and the situation, and eventually found himself in the place of authority he had dreamed about.

If Joseph can do it, you can, too.

God is a God of success.

---

5. Start thinking right.

The Bible says: "As a man thinks in his heart, so is he" (Prov. 23:7). The way you think determines who you are and what you will become.

How do you think? Do you think answers? Do you think victory? Do you face challenges with an open mind? Do you think *I will succeed!* Do you think God will help you make it through every challenge?

Have you ever wondered what you could accomplish if you knew you could not fail? Just think about that for a moment. What would you tackle if you knew that no matter what you did, you would not fail? You would go for it, and everything would work out because nothing else would make a difference. It would work.

Through the prophet Isaiah, God said, "Fear not; for I am with thee . . . I will strengthen thee" (Isa. 41:10). That verse will trigger the God-given power within you. It will help you change your habits of thinking and keep your mind free of paralysis. If your speaking is wrong, your believing is wrong. If your believing is wrong, your thinking is wrong. If your thinking is wrong, your speaking is wrong.

Begin thinking right. Begin thinking as if you are in charge. Begin thinking success for your life, your family, and your future. Keep your thought standards high, clean, and pure. You have a God-given ability to change your attitude, which in turn can change your circumstances.

6. Keep your eyes on your dream.

> *If you get your eyes off your dreams, your plans will get muddy and your goals will never be reached.*

You then will begin to see only negative situations. These will become like "soul termites," eating away at your dreams.

If you have failed, been disappointed, hurt or "stomped upon," don't let the past feed on your mind. If you do, you'll develop mental malignancy. Get up and go forward.

The Psalmist sang, "You will revive me . . . your right hand shall save me" (Ps. 138:7).

Your dream must burn in your heart. If it does, your dream will happen.

Your Dreams

What are your dreams? Are they of God? Will they bring about good? Do those dreams burn in your heart? Have you written them down? What choices are you making concerning these dreams?

Your future is a choice, a decision. With God's help, you can make your dreams come true.

List your dreams:

1.

2.

3.

4.

5.

2

Keeping Your Dreams on Track

D r. Martin Luther King said, "I have a dream." Those words have been repeated around the world again and again — in print, on radio and TV. Because he dared to both live and die for that dream, his life made a difference.

The Bible states in Proverbs 29:18, "Where there is no vision (or dream), the people perish." That's why you need to have dreams. Dr. King's dream was not only for himself but for others.

Jesus said, "I am come that they might have

life, and that they might have it more abundantly" (John 10:10). God intended that you lead a happy and full life, that you have dreams, and that you glorify Him.

Dreams are only dreams until you really believe in them and have the tenacity to hope and plan and work for them. A dreamer with a vision will create action to move forward.

> *Dreams are worthless if you only dream and don't take any action to reach a goal.*

Some people have dreams that go astray. When that happens, their plans get messed up, and their goals are never reached. The seeds of our God-given dreams need to be "watered" with well-laid out plans so that our goals can be reached.

How can you keep your dreams from being sidetracked? There are several ways.

Turn Failure into Success.

Many dreams have slipped through the cracks because of a single failure. Turn failure into success by putting God first in your life. God is a success in all He does. Dr. Robert Schuller advises you to "turn your scars into stars."

There is never a shortage of any kind with God. Take the example of air. No matter how much of it we breathe in, there is always more left.

It will not run out.

> *Many of the greatest accomplishments in history have been done against impossible odds because someone had a dream.*

When Thomas Edison was interviewed by a New York newspaper, he was asked, "How does it feel to fail 700 times trying to invent a practical filament for an electric light?"

He answered, "I have not failed, not even once. However, I have proven that 700 different ways won't work. When I eliminate all the other ways that won't work, I will find the way that works."

There were over 10,000 so-called failures, but Thomas Edison succeeded because he had a dream.

The events that appear to be failures in our lives actually bring us to a greater success. But we have to want to succeed. Many failures are due to weak will. I don't know anyone who succeeded without a will to succeed.

The "will" to succeed has pulled men out of their ruts and put them on the road to success. It has transformed unhappy, nervous, discontented individuals into dynamos. It has reawakened ambition, given confidence and courage, and overcome great weakness.

> **Some people are so busy failing they have no time to succeed.**

Louie Pasteur received a C grade in chemistry, but he developed the process of pasteurization of milk and a cure for rabies.

Einstein flunked high school math. We are told he never learned how to tie his own shoelaces. But his theories revolutionized science as we know it.

J.C. Penney was said to have been sent home from school because he wasn't smart enough to learn. He has now been dead for several years, and we are still sending him checks.

I facetiously told my daughter, Rebekah, the other day, "Don't mail him any more checks."

"Why?" she asked.

"Because we don't know where he went, and he doesn't need the money anyway, so why send it?"

At the age of 65, Colonel Harlan Sanders was broke. Today, his success in the Kentucky Fried Chicken business is known around the world.

Sally Bush, a God-fearing woman who lived over a century ago, had two stepchildren — a girl named Sarah, and a tall, gangling boy named Abraham. Every Sunday, she faithfully took her children by horseback to a country church that had a water bucket in the back of the church, a stove in the middle, a wooden pulpit, and backless benches. Abraham listened with interest as the old preacher prayed and preached long and loud.

Many years later, when this boy became a man, he stirred the nation with his speech on the Union and slavery. Abraham Lincoln quoted from the Bible. Where did he learn it? From a hard-shell Baptist preacher who knew little more than the Scriptures, but who said with faith and tear-filled eyes, "You can do it with God."

Now you know why Abe Lincoln was able to keep going after experiencing many failures:

1831 — He failed in business.
1832 — He was defeated for the legislature.
1833 — He failed in business again.
1836 — He had a nervous breakdown.
1838 — He was defeated for the house speaker.
1840 — He was defeated for the elector.
1843 — He was defeated for congress.
1855 — He was defeated for the senate.
1858 — He was defeated for the vice presidency.

But in 1860, Abraham Lincoln became the sixteenth president of the United States of America because he refused to give up.

> **God wants you to have dreams and take steps of faith toward those dreams.**

Did you know the 3M company was actually built by taking advantage of failures? In 1929, one of their engineers developed an adhesive tape to use as a seal for insulation. In practical applications, however, it didn't work. But when they experimented further with it, they found it did a great job of repairing torn paper. As a result, Scotch brand transparent tape was invented — almost by accident.

Today, Scotch tape is a 750 million dollar per year business. 3M took that failure and turned it into a success story. This company refuses to see failures; it only sees opportunities.

How about you? Do you see your failures as opportunities for success?

Don't Let Other People Destroy Your Dreams

Sharing your dreams with those who have no dreams can be dangerous. It may mean that you will face ridicule.

Joseph innocently and enthusiastically shared his dreams with his brothers. (See Gen. 37:1-11.) When they heard that they would one day bow down to their younger brother, they were outraged and hated him even more.

I know from experience that dreams can be almost destroyed by the ridicule of others. But this can happen only if we allow it. Don't let it happen to you. If your dreams die easily, maybe it wasn't really a dream; it was simply an idea.

When we were traveling as a singing family, our old motor coach wore out. It was always breaking down, and repair bills were eating into our budget. I decided I would get a new coach. It was a dream. I got a photo of the one I wanted and taped it on the wall of our old coach.

Then I met two kinds of people. Both would ask, "Why do you have that photo on the wall?"

I would say that I had a dream to get a new motor coach, a Silver Eagle. Some said, "Wow, do you know what they cost? You'll never be able to afford to buy one of those."

It didn't matter what the new coach would cost because we didn't have any money anyway. We simply needed a new coach.

I also met people who were positive and who said, "Wow, that is wonderful. You will get it."

One day a friend said, "Do you have a fund started for it?"

I said, "No."

He said, "Let me help you," and he wrote a check for one hundred dollars for the coach fund. He actually believed we would get the new coach.

Less than a year later, we had a brand new Silver Eagle coach. What a thrill! The doubters said it was a fluke. But I stayed excited about my dream and didn't let others tear me down.

When our oldest son got married, we got him a motor coach for his family so he could continue to travel and minister. You can have anything you believe for if you hold onto your dream no matter what people say.

Every dreamer has a vision.

I love the book by Dexter Yager called *Don't Let Anybody Steal Your Dreams*. He talks about associating with winners and how to develop a good self image and attitude.[1]

Choose your friends carefully. Don't let negative people talk you out of your dreams, steal them, destroy them, or even downgrade them.

Walt Disney dreamed of building a place where parents would take the family and have fun together. Walt's brother, however, tried to discourage him, saying it couldn't be done. It would be too expensive to maintain, he said, and parents would not pay just to visit with Mickey Mouse and Donald Duck. Walt Disney listened to all the reasons why he should not pursue the dream of building Disneyland and later Disney World.

Let me ask you, What is his brother's name? Do you know? Does it matter?

Walt Disney's dream came to pass and continues to grow even after his death because he refused to let someone destroy his dream.

Be Enthusiastic

A real dream produces a confidence and an enthusiasm that is the outward reflection of a deep belief. It doesn't matter what people say; a dream that is born of God will stay alive in your life.

Napoleon said, "Men of imagination and enthusiasm rule the world." Without those two ingredients, no cathedrals or skyscrapers would have been built, no races won, no battles fought, no empires founded.

When the flames of imagination and enthusiasm burn out, you feel as if you are in deep despair. That's when you need to be your own cheerleader. The Bible says that David encouraged himself in the Lord.

I don't really have a hold on the dreams in my life, they have a hold on me.

Have the kind of enthusiasm that comes from God. Get excited and bubble with excitement. Genuine enthusiasm is a companion to success. It will provide confidence, blast away obstacles, and spread like wildfire.

Every dreamer should have a vision, and "sell" that vision.

If you're a clothing salesperson, sell neatness, style, and fashion instead of just selling clothing. Likewise, if you are selling shoes, sell foot comfort. In the furniture business, sell a comfortable home. A bookstore should sell knowledge and the pleasure of reading. If you are selling refrigerators, sell better health because foods won't spoil. Selling farm machinery? Sell green fields and better crops.

The degree of enthusiasm you have in approaching your job, your studies, your ministry, or anything else will determine the level of success you achieve.

Maintain a Positive Attitude

Everyone I know who has a gigantic dream also has a great attitude. Have you worked on your attitude? This is important.

A story is told that hundreds of years ago, a king sentenced one of his slaves to be put to death immediately for committing a minor crime.

The slave begged the king to accept a bargain. He said, "If you will give me one year, from today, I will train your personal horse to fly. If I fail, then you can have me put to death."

The king thought, *What do I have to lose?* So he said to the slave, "We shall let you train my horse to fly. If you cannot accomplish it in one year, you shall be put to death."

Another slave said to the condemned slave, "You fool, why did you make such a foolish bargain with the king? You know you can't train his horse to fly."

The condemned slave answered, "I reason it this way. In one year the king might die, or he might forget our bargain, or he might have mercy and pardon me, or . . . I might teach that horse to fly."

So he dreamed of at least adding a year to his life and overcame the immediate death sentence.

A positive person sees all challenges as opportunities. When problems develop, dreaming helps them to go on.

> *If your thoughts are happy,*
> *you will become happy.*

Without a dream, however, there is nothing to live for; hope dies, and people give up. There is nothing to get excited about, to look forward to, to build for.

Don't let Satan rob you of positive thoughts. It's easier for the mind to become captive to negative ideas than to be encouraged with uplifting ones. The more negative thoughts you entertain, the more your positive thoughts will be smothered out. Self-pity, envy, greed, and boastfulness will grow like bad weeds and choke out what God really wants in your life.

If your thoughts are happy, you will become happy. If your thoughts are about God and about helping and encouraging others, your mind will create good, enthusiastic, God-centered thoughts about happy people.

Be Prepared to Modify Your Dreams

Some dreams are not practical, and a few are not possible in their original form. They may need some modification before they can actually come about.

Galileo dreamed that man would someday fly. In his time, and with the technology available to him, it was impossible. But today, man flies.

Please understand that dreams are general and have no deadlines. Just having dreams, however, doesn't make things happen.

> *God will never give you a dream without giving you the necessary abilities and the opportunities to achieve it.*

As a baby learns to walk, practice improves his skill. The first time he falls, we don't say, "All right, that's it. Don't ever try to walk again!" The baby may fall many times before he becomes proficient.

As we begin to walk with God, our ability is also improved with practice. A few stumbles teach us that we need to rely on Him and keep working to improve our walking.

Babies are not born knowing everything they will eventually need to know in order to survive. As they grow and learn, they become mature adults.

When we begin to walk with God, our footsteps sometimes falter. The longer we follow in His paths and the more we mature, the deeper our love for Him grows. We better understand His ways and His will, and our dreams change and mature as a result.

Stop Worrying about Things You Can't Change

Do you worry about things that can't be changed such as your past, your birthday, or your ethnic origin? Instead, change the way you think and react to situations, and you'll be able to channel that energy into overcoming the circumstances that keep you from dreaming.

Maybe you've heard someone say, "You have to know important people or be rich or have lots of education to get anywhere in life. What's going to be is going to be. This is just the way things are. I am the way I am."

But the way things are can be changed. God made you a free moral agent with the ability to choose and to change. Did you ever wonder if the way you are got you where you are?

Who we are right now has been molded by all the influences that have affected our lives: parental, religious, educational, social; plus what we ourselves have done or not done with those influences.

Two children can be born into the same family, have the same genetic background and the same environment. One becomes a pastor and the other ends up in prison. Why? Because of his/her dreams and the choices he/she makes.

At sixteen, Aristotle Socrates Onassis, the son of a tobacco merchant, was a penniless immigrant to Argentina. Of Greek extraction, Onassis and his family had lived in Turkey and then in Greece. He had worked as a dishwasher, waiter, and as a night telephone operator. He had listened in on calls in order to learn Spanish. Later, he started a small tobacco shop.

Then he heard that thirty freighters were for sale for twenty thousand dollars each. The ships were about ten years old and had cost two million dollars each to build. With the help of friends, he purchased six of them, sold four for a large profit, and operated the other two.

His dream was to be one of the richest men in the world. At twenty-five, in spite of a worldwide depression, he became a millionaire and kept working until he realized that dream.

> *There are plenty of splinters on the ladder to success, but you won't notice them unless you slide down.*

It's up to each person to keep his/her own dreams alive by feeding and watering them and never giving up on those dreams.

Be possessed by your dreams. Act upon those dreams. Plan for your dreams. Reach toward the goal of those dreams. Take action and be decisive. Your dreams have great possibilities.

3

Change Your Future Today

Norman Vincent Peale said, "Change your thinking, and your future will be changed." That's very true. We need to change how we think about situations.

Two men were swimming one day in a river. As they got out to get dressed, they saw a bear coming at them. They immediately rushed to get their clothes and shoes on. One of them asked the other, "Do you really think you're going to outrun that bear?"

His friend answered, "I don't have to. I

just have to outrun you."

Yes, our thinking needs to change. I love to see people think in a positive manner.

In 1954, Roger Bannister broke a world record and ran a four-minute mile. This was unheard of. Then in 1955, fifty-seven people broke Bannister's record; in 1956, over three hundred broke it. How do you think this was possible? Because other athletes said, "If Roger Bannister can do it, we can do it." Their thinking was changed.

Ten years ago, several fifteen-year-old Russian gymnasts defeated America's more experienced gymnastic team in world and Olympic competition. Today in the USA, we have ten year olds performing the same difficult stunts the Russians did then. Our coaches and gymnasts said, "If they can do it, we can do it, too."

> ### *"Change your thinking and your future will be changed."*

On a flight to another city, I sat next to Susie Barstow, a gymnastics coach who works for Phillips 66. She told me that she used to set goals for her youth to reach the state competitions. Then she would set regional, national, and international goals. The team, however, could never successfully get past the state levels.

Susie couldn't understand this until one day she realized the team only thought about the state competition. So she began to focus their thinking on the higher levels and make the state championships only a steppingstone. As their thinking changed, so did their achievements at the larger competitions.

How the Mind Works

I talked to a man one day who said we only use 10 percent of our mental capacity. When I asked him if this were really true, he assured me that it was. I countered, "Then you have a 90 percent chance of being wrong." He hadn't thought of that.

The human brain is a very complex computer. It contains approximately 100 billion nerve cells that begin to die at birth. These cells perform like tiny power plants and generate their own electrical power. They also produce hundreds of chemicals that affect our moods and reactions to situations.

The brain also has its own house-cleaning system. Scraper cells act like tiny vacuum cleaners, collecting dead and injured tissue and depositing it into the nearest vein to be carried away by the blood stream.

Our brain has two major parts: the conscious and the subconscious. The conscious mind controls and guides the subconscious. The subconscious guards your body's health, helps food digest properly, regulates heartbeat and breathing, and other involuntary functions.

Our mind, the seat of our consciousness, cannot be physically seen or touched. It is, so to speak, the computer program that is written on our brain. Like a computer, we draw our conclusions from the material fed into our mind.

> *The only truth that can set you free is the truth that you know.*

Unlike a computer, our minds have the ability to draw more than one set of conclusions from each situation. The conclusion we reach determines our attitude. Our attitude, then, determines whether we choose to react in a positive or negative way.

Life is said to be 10 percent what happens, but 90 percent is our reaction to what happens.

We often tend to deal not with actual reality but with our perception of reality. If a child has been frightened by a dog, he/she often grows up believing that all dogs are vicious.

The Monroe Clinic in Wisconsin made a study of common symptoms to find out how negative thoughts affected our bodies. Here are some of the percentages showing what they found:

Neck pain — 75 percent
Skin rashes — 30 percent
Gas — 90 percent
Headaches — 80 percent
Ulcer like pain — 50 percent

Dizziness — 80 percent
Constipation — 70 percent
Tiredness — 90 percent

Looks like what we think can determine how we feel.

Your mind is a storage facility. Computer operators have a saying, "Garbage in, garbage out." In other words, whatever you put into your mind is going to affect your thinking and your behavior. Computers store information on disks or diskettes; we store information in our conscious and subconscious mind.

Books, magazines, radio, movies, and television put thoughts into our minds that become our words, actions, character, and destiny. Suggestion is a powerful tool, both for good and for evil. That's why we need to be careful about choosing the kind of material we choose to program our minds.

Changing Your Input

Our minds are very sophisticated computers. They take the information we feed into them, merge it with the experiences of our lifetime, and feed back to us our response to any given situation. In order to have our lives changed, we often need to change the input.

How do you do that? Let me make a few suggestions:

1. Change what your ears hear and your eyes see.

We need to change what we choose to hear on the radio and see on television. There is so much garbage filling the air waves. The books and magazines we read should be carefully screened to make sure they do not tempt us to impure or unholy thoughts.

Remember, what you think about determines where you will end up.

> *Your life moves in the direction of your most dominant thoughts.*

An obsession with horror movies will fill your life with fear. An addiction to pornography will lead to sexual abuse. A love for sports will make you want to be an athlete. A desire to serve others will open doors for ministry.

2. Change what you do in your spare time.

You say, "I need to relax," so you turn on the TV. If you want to watch TV, monitor what you watch. If you can't control your viewing, you would probably be better off to get rid of the television.

If you want to be productive in your life, make sure what you do in your spare time helps you accomplish your dream. Stop wasting your time on things that don't matter.

If you want to be a basketball coach, spend

every waking moment learning the rules of the game and studying the techniques of successful coaches. If your dream is to win a scholarship to a prestigious college, use your spare time to study and develop your academic skills.

3. Change who you associate with.

If your friends are negative, cynical, and critical, find new friends. Associate with people of faith who know how to get results.

Many years ago in England, George Mueller had hundreds of children living in the orphanage he operated by faith. Many times there wasn't enough food to feed them all when mealtime came. The Muellers would gather the children around the table and pray. While they were praying, food would arrive at the door from some unexpected source.

Because of George Mueller's faith and devotion to prayer, the orphanage grew to house more than two thousand children.

During a trip to America, the ship on which Mueller was traveling was hit by a violent storm. Waves washed over the sides of the vessel, and everyone feared it would break apart.

The captain came to George Mueller's room and said, "Sir, I believe that we are going to go down within twenty minutes. I thought you might like to pray."

Mueller responded, "Yes, I would like to pray."

The captain said, "Sir, would you like me to pray with you?"

"No," Mueller said, "I know what you believe. You believe we are going down in twenty minutes. Leave me alone. I can't pray with someone who believes that we are going down. I must believe that when I pray, God will still this violent storm."

Mr. Mueller prayed, the storm subsided, and they made it safely to America.

> *God wants to change you*
> *and your thinking, but He*
> *needs your cooperation.*

Find people who believe like you believe and have the same dreams for their life. If you only associate with people who mainly live to party on the weekend, you'll be a party animal, too. Surround yourself with people who love to witness about Jesus, you'll be an evangelist, too. If your friends dream of becoming missionaries, you'll soon catch the vision and see yourself in faraway places.

4. Change your values.

Have you lowered your values and your standards to meet those of the world around you? Are you renting movies you wouldn't have dreamed of watching a few years ago? Does an occasional foul word slip out of your mouth? Are you only concerned about having the latest and greatest new toy — whatever it is at the time?

Do you care more about what other people think than about what God thinks? Do you place enough value on your family, your spouse (if you are married), your friends, your minister, your church attendance, your giving?

Remember that everything reproduces after its own kind. Don't just be average, run of the mill, or status quo. Have the courage to be different and value the things and people that really count.

5. Choose to change.

Say, "I choose to change now. I believe God will help me. I believe that answers will come my way. The dreams that God has given me are wonderful. I will put action to them, and lay plans to reach my goals."

> *You can reach goals if your thinking is changed.*

Years ago, when we started a contemporary band to reach unchurched young people, I was criticized by fellow Christians and pounced on by my friends. After a while, I began to wonder if God had really called me to do His work.

One day, as I was questioning God, I flipped on the TV, and the first voice I heard was Robert Schuller. He said, "You need to walk away from your yesterdays!" These words were like water in the desert . . . like air to a drowning man. My faith leaped up, and tears filled my eyes.

I said, "Yes, I will think differently. I will forget the criticisms and failures. I will go on!"

I did go on to a ministry that touched many young people. Today some of those who criticized me have seen the value of contemporary music and have formed their own musical groups.

How to Change Your Natural Thinking

When women marry, they think that their husbands will change. When men marry, they think that their wives will *never* change. Actually, they're both wrong. It's their thinking that needs to change.

Many potentially happy marriages, many potentially successful futures, many potential multi-million dollar businesses, many potential large churches have been hijacked by wrong thinking.

When the world thinks and talks divorce, you should emphasize the strengths of your marriage. When businesses around you are failing, work and pray and talk success. When your church is not growing as it should, help people find answers; and your church will reap a harvest.

You can reach goals if your thinking is changed. If you want to change your thinking, you have to reprogram your mind. "Do not be conformed to this world, but be transformed by the renewing of your mind, that you may prove what is the good and acceptable and perfect will of God" (Rom. 12:2). That's the secret.

> ***When you limit what you think you can do, you really limit what you can accomplish.***

The best way to renew your mind is to read your Bible every morning. As you read God's encouraging words, you will begin to think differently for the day. You will be able to tackle any challenge. It will bring a calmness to your spirit, and a calm person knows how to adapt, manage his schedule, and himself. It will help you keep from ruining the day with an explosive temper.

The Bible says, "The truth will set you free." But the only truth that can set you free is the truth that you know. Our minds need to be shampooed with God's Word.

When we change our thinking, miracles happen.

Abraham changed his natural thinking and began praying for a child (see Gen. 15:2-6). He even took things into his own hands and fathered Ishmael. But God answered, and Isaac was born (see Gen. 21:1-3).

Joshua changed his natural thinking, and made history. He commanded the sun and moon to stand still, and they did — for the space of a whole day (see Josh. 10:12-14).

Elijah changed his natural thinking, and his

prayer caused fire to fall from heaven and consume not only the sacrifice, but the wood, and the stones, and the water (see 1 Kings 18: 21-39).

King Darius changed his natural thinking. When he was forced by his own decree to cast Daniel into the den of lions, he declared, "Your God . . . is able to deliver you!" And God did (see Dan. 6).

Jesus changed the thinking of many people. He healed the sick, He cleansed lepers, He fed multitudes with almost nothing, and He even raised the dead.

Change your natural thinking, and many things in your life will change. God wants to change you and your thinking, but He needs your cooperation.

The Bible says we are to have the mind of Christ. Take the limits off yourself.

Kill the Monsters!

I like small children. They'll believe almost anything, and they like to make up stories and games.

My grandchildren love to play "monsters." When they are looking the other way, I will knock on the wall or under the table. Their eyes get big, and they yell, "Monsters!" We all know it's just a game.

They have discovered that the "monster" is really Papa, and there is no need to be afraid. This knowledge doesn't diminish the fun of the game. Real and pretend are somewhat interchangeable for a preschooler.

> ### *God will kill the monsters in our lives if we let Him.*

Recently, when I was visiting with a pastor who has a four-year-old son, I started my monster game and carried it a bit too far. At first he told me that ants would eat the monsters. I convinced him that the monsters had devoured the ants. Then it was mice and finally rabbits. My logic dealt with those, too, and as we parted for the afternoon, leaving him to believe the monsters were alive and well.

His mother later asked me to please take care of the monsters. It seemed that my young friend had been unable to take a nap because he saw them everywhere. That evening, it started raining so I told him that the monsters had drowned in the rain and washed away. His response was, "Praise the Lord!"

I couldn't help but think that it would be great if we adults could deal with our "monsters" as easily as I dealt with his. Many of us have monsters that we carry with us every day.

We have unfounded fears, feelings of worth-lessness, unreasoning anger, worry, unforgiveness, and other negative emotions that rob us of our ability to dream.

In order to deal with these things, we must deposit positives into our "mind bank," so that when the monsters begin to knock, we can make the proper withdrawal, and effectively "kill the monsters."

Reprogram Your Mind

In the book of Philippians, Paul wrote that we should think on things that are true, honest, just, pure, lovely and of "good report." He went so far as to tell these Christians to do what they had seen him do (see Phil. 4:7-8).

The apostle Paul faced "monsters" everywhere he went, yet Paul could say that God's peace kept his heart and mind. He had learned how to let God "kill the monsters" in his life.

I was working late at my office one night when Woody Clark, a good friend of mine and owner of Woodpecker Trucks, called. He asked, "What are you doing?"

I said, "I'm trying to work something out."

He retorted, "Have you ever thought about letting God work it out?"

I said, "Yes, but I'm . . . ."

Woody cut me off, saying, "God can take care of it."

I tried again. "I know, but . . . ."

He interrupted me again with, "God will handle it."

This time I got a little farther. "I trust God, but . . . ."

Woody said, "Go home, go to bed, rest in peace! Just shut up and prove that you trust Him. Don't make the need bigger than God."

I went home, got a good night's rest, and God worked the problem out. I thought, *God will kill the monsters in our lives if we let Him.*

If God is good, why must we sometimes face

negative challenges and experiences in our lives? The apostle Paul wrote that "all things work together for good." He didn't say that all things were good, but if we trust God, He will make things work for us and for His glory.

> ## *"Don't make the need bigger than God."*

There are a number of monsters that can plague us. Here are some of them, along with some Scripture references that should effectively kill them.

- **Confusion:** "I shall not be confounded" (Isa. 50:7). "God is not the author of confusion" (1 Cor. 14:33).

- **Discouragement:** "Let not your heart be troubled" (John 14:1). "Being confident . . . that He will perform it" (Phil. 1:6). "In due season, we shall reap" (Gal. 6:9).

- **Worry:** "Casting all your care on Him" (1 Pet. 5:7). "Peace I leave with you" (John 14:27).

- **Loneliness:** "I will never leave you" (Heb. 13:5). "I am with thee" (Isa. 41:10).

- **Temptation:** "The Lord knows how to deliver the godly out of temptations." (2 Pet. 2:9). "He is faithful ... to forgive our sins" (1 John 1:9). "Resist the devil, and he will flee from you" (James 4:7).

- **Anger:** "A soft answer turns away wrath" (Prov. 15:1). "Cease from anger" (Ps. 37:8).

- **Fear:** "God has not given us the spirit of fear" (2 Tim. 1:7). "The Lord is my helper, and I will not fear" (Heb. 13:6). "There is no fear in love" (1 John 4:18).

- **Sickness:** "Who heals all your diseases" (Ps. 103:3). "By his stripes we are healed" (Isa. 53:5). "I will restore health in thee" (Jer. 30:17).

- **Financial Challenges:** "I shall not want" (Ps. 23:1). "God shall supply all your need" (Phil. 4:19).

Are you facing other monsters? The answer to their defeat is to reprogram your mind with the Word of God. As our loving, heavenly Father, He wants to destroy the monsters that threaten His children.

If you continue to think like you've always thought, you'll always get what you've always got.

4

Raising Your Faith Expectations

The Bible states that faith in God will move mountains. Some people believe that, and some don't.

What is faith? How does it work? What changes do we need to make so it works for us?

The Bible defines faith as "the substance of things hoped for, the evidence of things not seen" (Heb. 11:1).

The eleventh chapter of Hebrews has been called the Faith Hall of Fame. It lists a number of Old Testament saints and the trials they overcame as they lived their lives for God. The chapter tells us of the purpose of faith, its plan, its promise, its power, and its proof.

When I speak of faith, I'm not speaking of a theological supposition. Real faith, in order to stand in a negative society — to succeed, to survive — is not based on theory, doctrine, theology, or denominational creed. No. It must be based on something that is impregnable, infallible, and cannot be shaken — the Word of God.

Faith is the biblical response to truth. It is your choice to believe truth. Just believing doesn't make something true. It is true, so we believe it.

New Age philosophy distorts the truth by saying we can create reality through what we believe. Faith doesn't create reality, it responds to reality.

> *It's not just what we believe,*
> *it's who we believe that*
> *makes a difference.*

If you harbor unbelief, you are taking sides against God.

I could never be an atheist. Why? Because I know that Someone makes a rooster crow and a hen lay eggs. Someone puts stripes on a zebra and keeps fish from drowning. Someone makes every cow in the world get up back feet first while all the horses get up front feet first. And the animals never make mistakes.

Someone brings in twenty-six waves to the minute on the seashore. It doesn't matter whether the waves are small or large, there are always twenty-six to the minute. Only God could do that.

God wants you to have dreams and take steps of faith toward those dreams. God is speaking, but are you listening? (See 2 Cor. 5:17 and Matt 9:29.)

Going Against the Odds

Have you ever noticed that life tends to respond to your outlook? Things will go badly when we expect them to.

Your faith may be tested to the limit, but you can go no farther than what you believe for. That is why you need to raise the level of your faith expectations. You can't finish in faith until you get started in faith.

When you have a crisis, raise the level of your faith expectations. When you really don't know what to do, raise the level of your faith expectations. Even when it seems that you have totally failed, raise the level of your faith expectations.

When negative people try to tear you down, raise the level of your faith expectation. When you feel you need proof to get through a challenge, remember you can believe God without proof.

Ignore the dedicated agitators. Raise the level of your faith expectations. If you're going to fail, you don't need help to do it.

You must understand that the eyes of faith see much differently than natural eyes. Faith expects answers. Faith turns negatives to positives.

> ## *No one can make you a failure without your consent.*

When you raise the level of your faith expectations, you will begin to believe against impossible odds. Conversely, when your mind disbelieves, you will find reasons to support your doubts.

Look at George Washington Carver, Helen Keller, and Christopher Columbus. Each faced a set of circumstances considered to be "impossible." They all believed. They all had dreams and knew how to raise the level of their expectations. And they each reached and exceeded their dreams.

Frank Gunsaulus was an ordinary minister who lived in Chicago about a century ago. But he had a God-given dream. He wanted to help young people who had no funds go to college.

In 1890, he ran a newspaper ad stating that he would preach on "What I Would Do if I Had One Million Dollars."

The small church was packed. After hearing the pastor preach, Philip Armour, owner and president of Armour Meat Packing Co., donated the million dollars. Frank Gunsaulus then established the Illinois Institute of Technology, which became a great center of learning.

Faith . . .
Never gives up,
Overcomes obstacles,

Forgives,
Is calm,
Never panics,
Uplifts,
Breeds hope,
Is positive,
Never criticizes,
Has confidence,
Creates a good atmosphere,
Creates a great attitude,
Has a balanced confession,
Doesn't get discouraged,
Takes every emergency leisurely,
Helps you zero in on your dreams.

I believe that God wants to help you. You can have purpose. You can change your world. You can be action oriented.

You can help build a new church. You can establish a business. You can take a risk. You can make it happen. You can touch lives. You can believe against impossible odds. Your age or socio-economic status don't matter. You can do it.

Rise above the procrastination, the indecision, the negative situations, and start turning your dreams into plans and your plans into goals.

> *Faith in God will turn you on, light your fire, flip your switch, and float your boat!*

Turning Dreams into Reality

I've been to East Berlin many times. What a dreary place. As we passed the checkpoints, we watched as the guards put mirrors under every vehicle to see if cars were transporting people illegally to the West.

The German guards, the guns, the wall and barbed wire fences, the graves and the crosses brought tears to my eyes. People had dreamed of freedom. Many had a dream to go to the free world. Even if it meant death, they wouldn't let loose of the dream of freedom.

Some rammed the wall with vehicles, hoping to break through. Others took their chances at night. They had a dream, and they had determination. They would rather die free then live under communism.

Shortly before I arrived on my first visit to Berlin, a young man had tried to swim across the river at night. He had a little plastic tube he breathed though, hoping that the guards wouldn't spot him. He swam a couple of feet beneath the surface of the water, very carefully and very slowly. When a guard saw movement and shot into the water, blood came to the surface. The young man's body floated to the side. He had a dream, and a goal, but the plan didn't work.

I have a photo of a sign that someone spray-painted on the Berlin Wall — probably at night. Although the paint ran, and the sign was rather crude, it expressed a dream. It read: "This wall will come down."

Faith makes dreams become reality.

How does faith make dreams reality? When the dream so possesses you that you cry out to God for the fulfillment of that dream.

One way to raise the level of your faith is to give thanks. If your dream is financial, remember that God is the eternal source and divine supplier of every need. Give thanks daily for the exact amount of your need.

Opportunities are always knocking at your door. Oil the hinges, and walk through. Be action oriented. Climb the ladder one rung at a time. Travel cross country one mile at a time. Break the barrier of limitations; jump higher hurdles.

The ship *Mayflower* traveled at the speed of two knots per hour. That's slow, but it kept going. It overcame many obstacles in order to reach the goal.

Keeping Your Dreams Alive

Satan is negative, and fear activates him. He is a failure, a deceiver, a loser, and a devourer. All that Satan has, or even claims to have, is stolen stuff. He wants to destroy you and any dreams you have so he can kill your faith.

Remember, God is success. He is supply oriented by nature. Because He is our Father, He wants to meet the needs of His children. Faith will activate God, and He can help you keep your dreams alive. But you have to do your part. Here's how!

> ### The size of your success will depend on the size of your dream.

1. Dream bigger dreams.

When you feel that your dream is impossible, dream bigger.

When you think you don't have "what it takes" and your confidence slips, maybe because of past failures, dream bigger.

When some one laughs at you or takes a cheap shot, dream bigger.

If you have a dream you can accomplish in your lifetime, it's too small a dream. Think about that.

We need to respond to our dreams and act on them. We can miss what God has for us when we don't step out and "walk on the water."

Whether you're a teenager or a senior citizen, remember this: *When* you do something doesn't matter; it's *doing* something that counts.

- Mozart wrote a symphony when he was six years old.
- Shane Gould won her first Olym-

pic medal at age twelve.

• Joan of Arc led an army when she was only seventeen.

• Ray Kroc at age fifty-seven founded McDonald's.

• Colonel Sanders began his Kentucky Fried Chicken franchise at age sixty-five.

• Grandma Moses didn't start painting until she was seventy-eight.

It has been said that you are as young as your faith, as old as your fears; as young as your confidence, as old as your doubts; as young as your dreams, as old as your despair.

No one grows old by living a certain number of years, we grow old only when we lose our dreams.

2. Make God your partner.

Develop your future with God as your partner. He gave you the dream in the first place.

Our primary dream should be to be like the Lord. When we get our lives in line with His will and His laws, our dreams will move forward in a positive way. Dreams often flounder when we neglect to make God our partner and ask His advice.

Some Christians make a real impact because their relationship with God affects every aspect of their existence. They may or may not be blessed with large amounts of material resources, but their efforts are directed toward fulfilling a dream of helping others.

Many missionaries have followed God-given dreams and spent their lives in remote areas where the visible results of their teaching were few. In the light of eternity, however, their success will rank with that of great evangelists like Moody and Billy Graham.

> *Real success is knowing what God wants YOU to do and doing it.*

There is a success cult in the world. In fact, I know people who will travel anywhere to hear a speaker talk about success and how to get it. They read all the bestsellers, listen to every tape, and follow any road that has a sign, "Success Just Ahead."

Although many people desire success, most have no real concept of what success is. They desire it because it gives them status and means lots of money, multiple homes, fancy cars, and security in life with lots of comfort and time to travel all over the world. These desires are natural tendencies. What I'm saying is, money isn't everything. It doesn't buy happiness.

But as Christians, we know that real success involves serving others, and it's not for just a privileged few. That kind of success is something we can all experience.

What is real success? Real success is knowing what God wants *you* to do and doing it.

3. Have the right motivation.

A salesman was releasing white balloons to attract a crowd to the business he was opening. A little boy came up to him and asked, "Sir, if you turn colored balloons loose, will they go up, too?"

The salesman smiled and answered, "Son, it's not the color on the outside that makes the balloon rise into the air, it's what's on the inside that sends it up."

Like the color of the balloon, *external* motivation in our lives often comes from outside sources, such as Christian speakers, books, tapes, and videos. These are very necessary, but their ability to motivate is only temporary.

Internal motivation flows from God and a strong desire to see a dream come into being. It is strengthened by *external* sources, but does not originate in them. God is our Motivator, and He becomes the driving force for our dreams.

We need to be motivated to do God's will.

God is the Giver, and man is the receiver. You were born to have dreams, to be successful, to be productive, and to worship God, our Creator. Start believing that.

Jesus said, "If you can believe, all things are possible" (Mark 9:23). Your dreams have great possibilities.

Believe in your dreams and let them burn in

your heart and mind. Add knowledge and action and faith in God, and you can make dreams come true.

Part II

Plans

5

God's Blueprint for Your Life

God has a plan. That plan involved giving His only Son for mankind so we could have eternal life. "For God so loved the world that He have His only begotten son, that whosoever believeth in Him should not perish, but have everlasting life" (John 3:16).

That is God's plan for the salvation of mankind. Short and to the point, but it cost Him the only Son He had. God was possessed by a unique sense of responsibility for us. What a commitment! What a plan! All laid out, and completely unchangeable.

> ### God also has a plan for you
> ### and your future.

He has already laid out the blueprint He has for you. Since God has a specific plan for your life, you need to get into partnership with Him. Commit your total self to Him and prayerfully seek to know God's plan for your life.

It doesn't matter what has happened in your life in the past. With God, there's always another chance. God will meet you where you are, pick you up, and help you get into His plan.

The woman at the well had lived a hard, immoral life, but Jesus accepted her where she was, and her testimony caused the city to believe on the Saviour (see John 4). Mary Magdalene had been a harlot, but Jesus changed her life, and today her name is a household word.

Because God is our source, our weakness doesn't affect Him. Your failure or success depends on you letting God work His plan in your life.

God made you for a reason. Remember, God placed you on this world for a purpose. He has a plan for you life. You're important to Him. It is no accident that you're reading this book. It's part of His plan for your life. Absolutely nothing happens by chance with God.

When you were born, God had a blueprint for your life. He wants you to succeed.

Nowhere Land

Satan will do everything within his power to keep you from developing plans. Why? Because he knows the value of God-given plans.

Today, many troubled young people don't succeed because they are an easy target for drugs, alcohol, and a destructive lifestyle. They have no dreams, no plans, and no goals — and their lives have no purpose.

I think it was the Beatles who sang the song, "He's a nowhere man, sitting in a nowhere land, making nowhere plans for nobody. He doesn't have a point of view. He knows not where he's going to. He's a real nowhere man with nobody."

What about you? Do you know the direction God wants to lead your life? Do you have a plan that you and the Lord have laid out together? Or did you lay out your own plan, and then ask Him to bless it?

> *No one plans to fail, but they often fail to plan.*

Plans bother some folks because they think it will cramp their style or stifle their creativity. Nothing could be further from the truth. Developing a plan for your future is the most creative task you will ever undertake. In fact, it will actually set you free to live a richer, fuller life.

Without a plan, you will never reach your

goals. Your life will drift into nowhere. If you have no plans, then circumstances, the challenges of the hour, unusual situations, and negative people will determine your priorities. You will never get out of low gear.

Why do people fail? Do they plan to fail? No one plans to fail, but they often fail to plan.

It has been said that 98 percent of all projects that fail, fail because of poor planning.

Why You Need a Plan

I have a friend who never makes any plans for the future. He makes no plans about going to heaven and no plans for his life or his family and no plans to attend church. Yet, he booked a pack mule two years in advance so he could ride it through the Grand Canyon in Arizona. Let's face it. We plan for the things that are important to us.

Planning is crucial to any project. You wouldn't think of taking a trip without some planning. The managers of a factory wouldn't try to build a new car without plans. You wouldn't begin a new home without an architect's plan.

When a congregation wants to build a new church, they need a blueprint of the design. They don't just buy a piece of land, get bulldozers, push some dirt around, pour a slab of cement, and have people gather some old boards and nails and start building.

They have a plan. Otherwise they would be totally frustrated, and nothing would be accomplished. The project would be a total failure.

> ***You will never accomplish
> more than you set out to
> accomplish or more than you
> plan to accomplish.***

Tell me, where are you when you see a parking lot both to the left and right of a building? Two glass doors open from the street into this brick building with large windows all around. When you enter, you walk on a tile floor, face a menu directly in front of you, and approach four cash registers.

You guessed it. You're at McDonalds. All McDonalds are built according to that plan, and it works. I was in one in Tokyo, and another in Africa; both were built the same way.

What about a building that has parking areas on either side and doors coming in from each side? As you enter, there is a brass rail, a menu above, but only one cash register.

Where are you now? That's right — Wendy's. They also have a plan, and it works for them. See how important plans are?

Now that you're convinced, where do you start? First, as we have discussed, you begin with a dream — the thing you want to accomplish. Then you begin to work toward that dream. If you know what you want, you can begin to plan for it. You will need direction and guidance, of course, but don't be afraid to start.

How do you begin to develop your plan? Let me give a few pointers.

Get God's Plan

What does God want for your life? Have you asked Him? Or do you want to set up your own plans? Plans need direction, and that direction comes from God.

Paul said in 1 Corinthians 9:26 "I do not run like a man running aimlessly." You will run aimlessly for sure without God in your plans.

For example, my ultimate goal is to spend eternity in heaven. But unless I make some plans to get there, I will never reach my goal. So I accepted Jesus Christ as my Saviour and made Him Lord of my life. He is the captain of my ship.

Two children were standing on the deck of an ocean liner, watching the waves. The little boy asked, "What makes this ship go?"

The girl answered, "It's the captain!"

"No, it's not," said the boy. "What do girls know about ships, anyhow? Come with me, and I'll show you what makes the ship go." He took her down to the engine room.

Later they were both again on the deck of the ship. Someone screamed, "Man overboard!" A passenger had fallen into the ocean and was struggling to keep his head above water.

The captain ordered the engines to stop, and they stopped. He ordered the engines to reverse, and they did. The gigantic ocean liner headed for the drowning man. The captain ordered them to throw him a lifeline. They did, and the man was saved.

The girl said, "See, I told you that the captain runs the ship."

Let Christ run your life, and you'll never wonder where you are going. Give Him a chance to show you what His plan actually is. He has a plan, a blueprint, and all the answers for you.

> ### *God wants you to get involved in His plan.*

If you're not yet sure what God has in mind for your life, let me give some plans you can put into effect immediately.

1. Plan to *be* what God says you can be.

Paul wrote to the Roman church that "we are more than conquerors" (Rom. 8:37).

The apostle John says, "Greater is He that is in you than he that is in the world" (1 John 4:4).

You say that you are weak, and not worthy? God's Word says that He makes us that way so His "strength can be made perfect in our weakness" (2 Cor. 12:9). What more can we ask?

2. Plan to *do* what God says you can do.

Jesus told us to "ask, and you shall receive" (Matt. 7:7-8). He said that we could "have whatever (we) say" (Mark 11:22-23). And He also said that those who believe in Him would do "greater works" than He did.

When Jesus spoke those words, He was speaking to a group of mature people, and He wasn't giving them license to do foolish or unbalanced things. Just the opposite. He was giving them power to do great things for Him.

3. Plan to *have* what God says you can have.

Plan to pray and receive answers.

We can have God's eternal life (see John 3:16), and everlasting life (see 1 John 5:10-13). We can have "divine nature" (see 2 Pet. 1:3-4). He has given us the power to overcome dangers and evils (see Luke 10:19 and Mark 16:17-18).

Yes, God has plans. Proverbs 8:29 states, "I was there when you made the blueprint for the earth and the ocean" (LB). He doesn't need a new plan, but He does want you to get involved in His plan.

Pray God's Plan

After God gives you direction for His plan for your life, you need to soak those plans in prayer.

When you depend on man, you only get what man can do for you. If you rely on a good education, you will get what education can do. But when you depend on prayer, you will receive what God has for you.

Do you want to experience the thrill of answered prayer? Then your daily talking must change. Stop using words of discord or limitation or luck or bad luck or bad times. Begin to speak inspiration, blessing, and healing to others. Your words have authority, and mixed with prayer, they can move mountains.

Remember when Jesus was at the tomb of Lazarus calling, "Lazarus, come forth" (John 11:43). It was a good thing He said Lazarus, or all the dead would have come out. Lazarus rose, came out, and met his sister and his friend.

Use words of healing and blessing for others. Those you are praying for may not know it at the time, but it doesn't matter (see Isa. 50:4).

> *When you depend on prayer, you will receive what God has for you.*

As you pray, don't say, "Oh, God, I'm in a mess. It's a hopeless situation. I'm sunk." Instead pray, "I am your child, and you are my God. I thank you for the blessings that have come my way. I'm expecting good things to happen to me. I stand on your Word and believe your promises. I believe my life will be blessed in every way."

Every morning I say:

1. Today is the greatest day of my life.
2. I will bless others today.
3. God will meet my needs, spiritually, physically, emotionally, and financially today.

4. God has a good plan for my life.

You know what you want, what your dream is, and that is why the plan will work for you. You never accept defeat.

The Bible is filled with examples of what earnest prayer can accomplish. Abraham interceded for Sodom, and Lot was delivered before God destroyed that wicked city (see Gen. 18:23). Moses interceded for the Israelites, and God spared them (see Exod. 32:31-32). The prophet Samuel prayed for Israel, and "the Philistines were subdued" (see 1 Sam. 7:5-12).

> *Jesus knew the importance of praying even as you plan.*

Jesus, who is our example in all things, began His ministry with prayer (see Luke 3:21). His prayers are recorded throughout the Gospels. He prayed as He approached His crucifixion (see John 20 and Luke 22:42), and even prayed on the cross.

Be Joyful as You Plan

Be filled with joy as you make plans. If you aren't enjoying the process, you won't have thoughtful, well-laid out plans.

Years ago, a man traveling through Mississippi called out from a train window to a man at a station and asked, "Is there anybody in this town enjoying their religion?"

The old man replied, "Them that's got it is!"

God wants to replace the negative things in our lives with positive ones.

Truth replaces error.

Peace replaces anger.

Love replaces hate.

Faith drives out fear.

Joy displaces sadness.

His strength replaces our weakness.

Hope overcomes despair.

The broken parts of our life can be repaired.

So be joyful, and you will lay out great plans.

6

Making Your Plans Work

You have dreams, and now you're working on the plan. With a strong sense of purpose and God-given energy, you can accomplish what you intend to accomplish.

When you want something strongly enough, a dream burns in your heart, and you will know *no* limitations. You will take risks at times. You will go up against tough circumstances. You will give up something you know for something you believe is better.

You know what you want, and what your plan is.

Most salesmen plan to make so many calls per day or so many sales per week. They have dreams that burn within them, and plans to reach their goals. They listen to tapes about how to close the sale, read books about successful marketing, and attend seminars on getting to the top. They check their plans over, then evaluate and re-evaluate those plans. That's important for people who are going someplace in life.

If you have a business, you need a plan. If you have a ministry, you need a plan. If you want church growth, you need a plan. Your personal life also needs a plan. With a plan you will achieve goals and see things happen in your life.

> *When you want something strongly enough, a dream burns in your heart, and you will know no limitations.*

Let's say you want to win people to the Lord. To accomplish your goal, you must set aside so much time per week to go witnessing door to door, making telephone contacts, or whatever. Once you have a plan, stick with it.

What about a plan for your family? Do you want to grow together spiritually? Plan family devotions for a certain time every evening.

What about your spouse? Do you want to make more time to spend together? Plan to date him/her once a week.

How about your children? Do you want to develop meaningful relationships with them? Plan to spend special time with each child every week.

What about your own life? Do you want to mature as a Christian and find God's will for your life? You will need a plan and the tools to accomplish it. Make a list of books you want to read. Develop a plan for daily Bible study. Plan to attend seminars and conferences where God's Word is being taught.

To make sure your plans will continue to work for you, here are a few pointers.

Don't Procrastinate

All the well-laid plans in the world are useless unless we act according to those plans. Procrastination is a major enemy of progress.

In the light of eternity, life is short, and the things we want to do must be done without delay.

The average lifetime is approximately 70 years. That's a little less than 25,600 days.

It will take some time to grow up, so by the time you are 20, you will have about 18,250 days remaining.

When you are 30, there are 14,600 days left to accomplish your goals.

At 40, the balance has decreased to about 11,000 days.

By 50, you are down to 7,300.

And at 60, only 3,650 are left.

I'm not ignoring the fact that many people live well beyond 70, or that much can be accomplished after that age.

> *Procrastination is a major enemy of progress.*

If you have no dreams, no goals, but are just putting in time, these numbers may be a relief; for those who are reaching to achieve specific things in life, they are a challenge.

Time is a resource that is not renewable. It cannot be hoarded, it can only be used or wasted. Don't let time be your enemy, make it your friend, and deal with it wisely.

Be a Front Seat Planner

When I'm traveling, I'm often picked up at the airport by my hosts. If the ride is over an hour or so, I like to ride in the front seat. I hate to sit in the back seat of a two-door car because the folks in front will soon forget about you.

Back there, you have no door handles, and on many cars, your window won't even roll down. The front seat folks have to let you out — if you get out at all. You have no control over the radio or tapes. That is up front, and they play whatever they like. They also have the controls for the air conditioner and the heater. Your weather is the way they set it.

If you were in a collision, they have air bags

while you have your face aimed into the back of the front seat. If you get hit from behind, they have the headrest, but your head may go through the back window.

> *We need to be in a position to influence the things that happen to us.*

After riding a while, you soon realize that they are totally ignoring you, and you are a second class passenger. You decide to make contact with other back seat occupants. When a car pulls up beside you at the red light, you look out your window and wave at the back seat people in the next car. You know how they feel. They smile faintly and wave back as if they understand.

So for longer trips, my plans are to ride in the front seat.

It's important to have plans. Be a front seat planner.

In our lives, we also need to "ride in the front seat." We need to be in a position to influence the things that happen to us. God is driving the car, but our choices make a difference in the quality of the ride. He doesn't put us in the back seat where we are carried along without even the ability to open the door. He has given us the ability to choose, and He expects us to make our choices within the boundaries of His master plan.

Be Flexible

If I am planning to drive from Seattle to Florida, there are several possible routes. I can first drive south to California, then turn east and travel through Arizona and Texas (among other states). Or I can first drive east to Chicago before I head south and not go through either California or Arizona. Several other good routes also exist.

My eventual choice of route will probably depend upon such factors as the weather and if there are people and places I would like to visit on my way. No single route is the only good one when I start.

The closer I get to Florida, however, the fewer options I will have. If I am in Mobile, Alabama, only one logical route exists. Any side roads that I choose will definitely slow me from my goal.

This same premise carries over into the general planning process. Know what you wish to accomplish, look at several methods of achieving it, then get started. There are often several equally valid methods or routes to use in reaching your goal.

Early in the planning, be as flexible as possible. There may be some alternate routes, roadblocks, detours, or construction, but we must keep moving forward within the plan.

Let me give you an example. You should attend church regularly. But, if your house catches fire about the time you were planning to go to church, forget the church, and save the house. That may be an exaggerated example, but it makes the point. Be flexible.

The more you learn about planning, the more you will plan, and the less time it will take to reach your goals.

> *Early in our planning process, this flexibility is fine, but as we get closer to our goals, it becomes necessary to commit.*

Stick to the Plan

You may say, "I have plan B if plan A doesn't work out." Early in our planning process, this flexibility is fine, but as we get closer to our goals, it becomes necessary to commit. The time comes when we must get rid of plan B, or plan A never will work.

Let's say you are planning to build a doghouse, and have never pounded a nail. You begin by looking at several doghouses, then pick the style you like. Numerous books show you in a step-by-step manner how to build a doghouse and give you a guide as to the necessary tools and materials. If you follow the instructions in the book, you will soon have a usable doghouse. Once you have decided which doghouse you are building, you need to stick to that plan.

When a seamstress sews a garment, she has a pattern to follow. She may be competent enough to make some minor variations on the pattern, but she will put it together in an orderly manner because she knows what she is making. Although she had options when she began, once the material is cut out, she is committed to that pattern.

Once you have decided on a plan of action, commit yourself to it, and don't waver. God will reward your faithfulness.

> *Don't blame fate for failures or credit luck for successes.*

Plan to be a Winner

A loser will say, "I will believe it when I see it." A winner says, "I will believe it without seeing it, because I know all thing are possible."

Winners:	*Losers:*
Are part of the answer.	Are part of the problem.
Have a plan.	Have an excuse.
Say, "Let me help you."	Say, "That's not my job."
See an answer.	See a problem.
Say, it's difficult, but possible.	Say, it's possible, but too hard
See the positive side.	See the negative side.

Fall down, but get up.

Fall down and say, "Somebody pushed me."

Never give up.

Quit.

> *The first step in accomplishing the impossible is refusing to believe that anything is impossible. That's where faith comes in.*

Faith is simply saying "yes" to God's Word. Faith is believing the impossible. Faith is believing without proof. "Faith is the substance of things hoped for and the evidence of things not seen" (Heb. 11:1). It's easy to believe something you can see. Believe what you can't see. Make plans to believe.

"Without faith," the Bible states, "it is impossible to please God" (Heb. 11:6).

Winners are on the building crew; losers are on the wrecking crew.

In your business, your church, and even your family, you are either on the building crew or wrecking crew. If you're on the building crew, you give, you go, you tell the good news, you serve, you help, you bless, you sacrifice.

If you're on the wrecking crew, you tear down, you criticize, you grumble, nothing is ever right. You won't give, you won't serve, you won't help, you won't go out of your way to sacrifice. You are negative, you jump from one thing to another and are never very happy because you are unhappy with yourself.

A losing mentality can be turned into a winning mentality. People don't set out to be losers in any life situation. You never hear someone say, "I'm starting a new business. In a year, we will lose our home and be bankrupt."

Make plans to be a winner.

Winners know they are not perfect. They recognize their weaknesses but have learned to maximize their strengths. They believe in the path they have chosen, and even when the going becomes difficult, they refuse to let fear control them.

Take responsibility for your actions. Don't blame fate for failures or credit luck for successes. Learn to carve the ordinary into the extraordinary.

Have faith. Be persistent. Adopt a never give up spirit and a good attitude. Be someone who has learned to climb over failures and challenges.

Bury negative attitudes because the ideas that you yield yourself to will become your master. Be a person who loves, gives, goes, serves, shares, helps, and plans. Be a winner!

---

*Learn to carve the ordinary
into the extraordinary.*

Your Plans

Make them flexible as you begin, but firm them up as you head toward the goal.

1.

2.

3.

4.

5.

6.

7.

7

Plan to Succeed

Without a plan, it's easy to get side-tracked by things that seem to be important but have little to do with achieving your original dream. The following parable puts this thought into perspective.

The Fishermen

Now it came to pass that a group existed who called themselves fishermen. And lo, there were many fish in the waters all around. In fact, the whole area was surrounded by streams and lakes filled with fish. And the fish were hungry.

Week after week, month after month, and year after year, these who called themselves fishermen met in meetings and talked about their call to fish, the abundance of fish, and how they might go about fishing.

Year after year they carefully defined what fishing means, defended fishing as an occupation, and declared that fishing is always to be a primary task of fishermen.

Continually they searched for new and better methods of fishing and for new and better definitions of fishing. Further they said, "The fishing industry exists by fishing as fire exists by burning."

They sponsored special meetings called "Fishermen's Campaigns" and "The Month for Fishermen to Fish." They sponsored costly nationwide and worldwide congresses to discuss fishing and to promote fishing and hear about all the ways of fishing such as new fishing equipment, fish calls, and whether any new bait was discovered.

> *The plea was that everyone should be a fisherman and every fisherman should fish.*

These fishermen built large, beautiful buildings called "Fishing Headquarters." The plea was that everyone should be a fisherman and every fisherman should fish. One thing they didn't do, however: *they didn't fish.*

In addition to meeting regularly, they organized a board of directors to send out fishermen to other places where there were many fish. All the fishermen seemed to agree that what was needed was a board that could challenge fishermen to be faithful in fishing. The board was formed of those who had the great vision and courage to speak about fishing, to define fishing, and to promote the idea of fishing in faraway streams and lakes where many other fish of different colors lived.

Also the board hired staff members and appointed other boards and held many meetings to defend fishing and to decide what new streams should be thought about. But the staff and board members *did not fish*.

Large, elaborate, and expensive training centers were built whose original and primary purpose was to teach fishermen how to fish. Over the years, courses were offered on the needs of fish, the nature of fish, where to find fish, the psychological reactions of fish, and how to approach and feed fish.

Those who taught had doctorates in fishology. But the teachers *did not fish*. They only taught fishing. Year after year, after tedious training, many were graduated and were given fishing licenses.

Some spent much study and travel to learn the history of fishing and to see faraway places were the founding fathers did great fishing in the centuries past. They lauded the faithful fishermen of years before who handed down the idea of fishing.

Further, the fishermen built large printing houses to publish fishing guides. Presses were kept busy day and night to produce materials solely devoted to fishing methods, equipment, and programs to arrange and to encourage meetings to talk about fishing. A speakers bureau was also provided to schedule special speakers on the subject of fishing.

> *Many who felt the call to be*
> *fishermen responded. They were*
> *commissioned and sent to fish.*
> *But like the fishermen back*
> *home* **they never fished.**

Many who felt the call to be fishermen responded. They were commissioned and sent to fish. But like the fishermen back home *they never fished*. Like the fishermen back home they engaged in all kinds of other occupations. They built power plants to pump water for fish and tractors to plow new waterways. They made all kinds of equipment to travel here and there to look at fish hatcheries.

Some also said they wanted to be part of the fishing party, but they felt called to furnish fishing equipment. Others felt their job was to relate to the fish in a good way so the fish would know the difference between good and bad fishermen. Others felt that simply letting the fish know they were nice, land-loving neighbors was enough.

After one stirring meeting on "The Necessity

for Fishing," a young fellow left the meeting and *went fishing*. The next day he reported that he had caught two outstanding fish. He was honored for his excellent catch and scheduled to visit all the big meetings possible to tell how he did it. So, he quit his fishing in order to have time to tell about the experience to the other fishermen. He was also placed on the Fishermen's General Board as a person having considerable experience.

> *Is a person a fisherman if year after year he never catches a fish?*

Now it's true that many of the fishermen sacrificed and put up with all kinds of difficulties. Some lived near the water and bore the smell of dead fish every day. They received the ridicule of some who made fun of the fishermen's clubs and the fact that they claimed to be fishermen *yet never fished*.

They wondered about those who felt it was of little use to attend the weekly meetings to talk about fishing. After all, were they not following the Master who said, "Follow me, and I will make you fishers of men?"

Imagine how hurt some were when one day a person suggested that those who didn't catch fish were really not fishermen, no matter how much they claimed to be. Yet it did sound correct. Is a person a fisherman if year after year he never catches a fish? *Is one following if he isn't fishing?*[1]

The Three-Point Fishing Plan

My father taught me three things about fishing:

1. Go where the fish are.

If you plan to catch fish, go where the fish are. Don't get up at four o'clock in the morning on a cold day, get all dressed, and go stand on a river bank unless you want to catch fish. If you don't plan to catch fish, stay at home, and drop your line in the bathtub.

So as Dad said, "Go where the fish are."

2. Don't scare them before you catch them.

As a boy, I used to throw rocks in the water.

Now if the plan is to actually catch fish, we can't scare them. After you catch them, you can laugh at them, or make faces at them, smile at them, sing to them, holler at them, or try to teach them Hebrew. It doesn't matter after you catch them. They are now in the boat or the net.

3. If your bait isn't working, change it.

Some church folks say, "This is the way we have always done it before. We always sang out of the hymn book, we didn't sing choruses or use an overhead projector. We always use these cloth bags instead of offering plates. We always use the King James Bible, not those new versions. The last pastor didn't do it that way! Why change now?"

But if it isn't working, if you're not making an impact in your area, maybe you should change bait.

> *You can change your methods without changing your principles.*

Changing in Mid-Stream

You can change your methods without changing your principles. That's what Jesus teaches in the fifth chapter of Luke. Jesus also had a three-point plan:

1. Scrap your old program.
2. Don't ask God to bless what you are doing. Instead, do what He is blessing.
3. Make plans to reach your goals.

Jesus was at Lake Gennesaret, and He had just finished speaking to the people when he turned to Simon Peter and said thirteen famous words, "Launch out into the deep and let down your nets for a drought."

Jesus knew that Simon had failed. He knew he had fished all night without catching any fish. Jesus didn't discuss it, or even mention it. It was a past failure that was worthless to worry about. He didn't even ask Simon if he wanted to go fishing.

Simon also knew he had failed the night before, and he began to make excuses, as many do. He talked about the failure. Even with Jesus in the boat, I'm not really sure Simon expected to catch fish.

Let's consider the approach that Jesus took:
Jesus told him *what to do* — to go fishing.
He told him *how to do it* — to let down his nets.
He told him *where to do it* — out in the deep.
He also told him *he would be a success.*

He had the whole plan laid out for Simon Peter. Because Simon decided to follow the plan, he was a success.

If I drive from Yakima to Seattle, the road is already laid out. But it is shorter "as the crow flies." So why don't I take off over the river and through the woods? I could say, "I don't care what others have done, I know a short cut. I'll do it my way." If I try it my way, I just plain won't get there.

Jesus was saying to Simon, "Your plan was a total flop. Now follow My plan and be a success. Scrap your plan and do it My way." Simon did, and he succeeded.

If your program and plan isn't working, maybe you need to listen.

You have heard it said, "Don't change horses in mid-stream." But I say:

> *"If your horse is dead, get off it and get another one!"*

To be a fisherman, you have to catch fish. It

doesn't matter if you have a boat, how much tackle and equipment you have, or if you live by the lake. You must catch fish to be considered a fisherman.

You will be as astonished as Simon was when he caught a boatload of fish. He decided to follow the Lord's plan.

God's plans work. He knows where the "fish" are today. Follow His plan, and you'll be a success. God is your source.

Part III

Goals

8

How to Set Attainable Goals

What are your immediate goals? Can you define where you'd like to be at the end of this year and five years from now?

> *Goals should be specific, solid, and serious. They should have deadlines.*

I have goals for one year, five years, ten years.

I even have lifetime goals. Research has shown that people who set goals are happier than those who do not. Even senior citizens should have goals.

As the Bible says, we are not just beating the air, we can actually have goals. Paul said in Philippians 3:14, "I press toward the mark (a target) of the prize of the high calling of God in Christ Jesus."

> **A goal is a dream in action,
> with a purpose.**

Some people think that ideas are goals. Not so. A goal is a dream in action, with a purpose. You cannot reach a goal if you don't have one. You can't hit a target if a target is not there. You're wasting your time if you don't have a mark to shoot at. You must have a goal.

You don't go to the airport and just buy a ticket to wherever. A ship doesn't just drift across the ocean.

I have read that 95 percent of Americans have no goals in life, and 100 percent of those never achieve them. Without goals, people have nothing to live for.

Why don't most people set goals? Here are some possible reasons:

1. They don't really have the faith to set them.
2. They don't know how to exercise a plan.
3. Some people are just too lazy.

4. They have a "don't care" attitude. They feel that the effort is just too great.

5. They might have to work at their goals.

6. Many people think they are too busy. Because they never set goals, they are too busy doing things that never get them anywhere. As a result, they run in circles.

7. They have failed before.

8. They really don't know how to set a goal.

A God-Given Instinct

Even the animals have goals.

Years ago, a group of scientists were doing some experiments with moths. A single female moth from a rare species was put in a room four miles from a male of the same species. They released the male, and within a few hours, he was flapping his wings against the window of the room that housed the female.

How did the male moth realize his goal of finding the female? All I can say is that God knew where to send him.

Birds have a goal of finding enough food to stay alive.

We had seen no birds around our house until my friend, Mel, threw bread out for them. Shortly, the backyard was full of birds who had come to eat it. My friend could have thrown out wood chips, and the birds would not have responded. Why?

Because food is their goal.

> ### Your future begins right now — with your goals.

After researchers tag salmon in the streams feeding into the Columbia River, the fish are released and swim downstream to spend four years in the Pacific Ocean. When they are ready to spawn, the salmon return to the same stream where they were tagged. How is their goal reached? By God-given instinct.

Dogs have been known to travel many miles to return home. How do they reach their goal of returning to the exact house they left?

If "dumb" animals have sense enough to reach their instinctive "goals," shouldn't we also have the sense to set and reach ours?

Be Specific

If you have God-given dreams that you'd like to accomplish and have well-laid, flexible plans to see those dreams fulfilled, you are now ready to set specific goals for your life. Your future begins right now — with your goals. They will give you a target to shoot for. As the apostle Paul said, "I press toward the mark."

Always remember that Satan wants to defeat you. He wants to diffuse your enthusiasm, and he will undermine your goals. Write your goals down on paper. Have specific goals. Know exactly what you want. Don't just leave it to chance.

You must be clear about what you want and where you want to go. Then you will have excitement and energy to help you reach your goal. If your goals are small, if you think small, you may develop a poverty complex. Many people who have lived through a period of recession or depression are never able to get beyond that period in their thinking. Even though their financial situation may be quite prosperous, they still live as though they were nearly penniless.

When Jesus passed through Jericho, a blind man heard the commotion and asked what was happening. When they told him that Jesus was passing by, he began to call out persistently, "Jesus, son of David, have mercy on me."

Jesus stopped and commanded the man to be brought over to Him. He asked, "What do you want Me to do for you?"

The blind man answered, "I want to receive my sight." He was specific.

Jesus replied, "Receive your sight; your faith has saved you."

Immediately the man could see and followed Jesus. The blind man had a specific goal — sight.

Jesus knew what the man needed, and He didn't really need to ask. But He wanted the blind man to be specific.

> *Goals should be specific,*
> *solid, and serious. They*
> *should have deadlines.*

When our kids were small, they would stand around whining and pulling at us. My wife or I would said, "What do you want? Tell me."

"I want a drink of water."

"Then ask for water. Say 'Please, may I have a drink.'" And we gave them a glass of water.

That's what Jesus did. He made the blind man verbalize his need. When the Lord asks us a question, it isn't because He doesn't know the answer. He wants an admission of need from us.

That's why it's important to have specific goals. When your goal is clearly defined — what you need, when you need it, where you want to go — you'll generate the energy and excitement needed to reach it. Success, winning, and reaching a goal are really a decision.

Winners Set Goals

Winners set goals. Winners don't quit, and they don't understand those who do.

I love being around our friends, Jim and Connie Agard, because they have goals and they have achieved goals. They have set goals and they have gone beyond their original goals, and they keep going. Jim and Connie see the overall picture: **the dream, the vision, the plan, and the goal.**

The Wright brothers' goal was to make a vehicle that would fly. Did they succeed? Not on the first try, but they didn't give up.

Wisdom is knowing what to do, skill is knowing how to do it, and success is doing it.

One day a very important machine in a factory broke down. The repair crew spent several days attempting to determine the problem and get it working again. Employees stood idle, and production was halted. Finally, in desperation, an outside consultant was called in to help.

The man walked around the machine several times as the crew explained what the machine had sounded like just before it quit. The consultant took a piece of chalk from his pocket and marked a small "x" on the machine. He then reached for a hammer and hit the machine on the "x" with a considerable amount of force.

"Turn it on; it'll work now," he said. Someone flipped the switch, and the machine whirred to life. Production resumed as employees returned to their places along the assembly line.

At the end of the month, the factory received a statement for the consultant's work. It totaled $500, and was itemized:

Hitting the machine	$1.00
Knowing where to hit	$499.00
Total	$500.00

That man knew what to do, how to do it, and got paid doing it!

> *Wisdom is knowing what to do, skill is knowing how to do it, and success is doing it.*

Henry Ford's goal was to make the "horseless carriage" available to everyone, and he knew how to do it. That's why you can afford to buy a car today.

Babe Ruth, one of the greatest home run hitters in baseball, struck out more often than any other player, but he kept on swinging. His success required that he consistently put himself in jeopardy of failing, but instead of defeating him, it motivated him.

Tough challenges, failures, and disappointments can help you jump hurdles, get over the top, and believe for an answer. Progress happens one step at a time.

The distance between losing and winning, between defeat and victory, between failure and success is not always that far. Success is just getting up one more time than you get knocked down.

Success doesn't require a super intellect. It does require a dream, with plans to reach a specific goal.

Set Goals Out of Reach, but within Sight

If your goals are your number one priority, you will find time and exert effort to make them happen. If you want real financial freedom, you will find a way to cut down on unnecessary spending. You won't make things worse by buying extravagant items or taking expensive vacations. You will find a way to pay off your bills. You will set goals.

Goals should be out of reach but within sight. I cannot reach a goal that I cannot see. I have to see the target before I can hit it. So I set my goals within sight but out of easy reach.

A common mistake is to set goals too high and then get discouraged because you can't reach them. Don't say, "I'm going to go out and win ten thousand people to the Lord this month." If you've never won three people to the Lord in your lifetime, how are you going to win that many in one month?

> *Goals should be out of reach*
> *but within sight.*

In 1959, the University of Minnesota football team finished dead last in the Big Ten Conference. In the spring of 1960, Murray Warmath, the head football coach, saw the importance of setting goals. He actually believed it could shape the abilities of the team. He called the players together and said, "Our goal is to win the Big Ten title and become eligible for a Rose Bowl invitation."

By setting a goal, each practice and each game had meaning. This team amazed the sports world when they tied for the Big Ten title and were named the number one team in the nation. And, yes, they did play in the Rose Bowl.

If you set your goals too low, there will be no challenge and, therefore, no excitement in reaching the goal. Establish goals, accompanied by sensible standards of self-expectation, and you will be challenged in a positive way, whether or not you exactly reach your goal. Let me give you an example.

Roger Maris wanted to break Babe Ruth's home run record of sixty during a single season. His first try only netted him fifty-nine, but he went on later to set a new goal. Even though he didn't achieve his first goal, his game benefited from the goal setting.

Set high but sensible goals that can be reached. Your goals are only as worthy as the effort required to achieve them.

Don't Be a Prairie Chicken

When Western Union was negotiating with Thomas Edison to purchase a ticker that he had invented, they told him to name a price. After Edison and his wife had talked it over, they agreed that $20,000 was fair.

When he went back to Western Union, he began to think that $20,000 was an exorbitant amount, so when they asked him, "How much?" he stood speechless. An officer of the company broke the silence with, "Well, how about $100,000?"

Again I'll say, if your goals are small, you may develop a poverty complex. Many people who have lived through an economic recession or depression are never able to get beyond that period in their thinking. Even though their financial situation may be quite prosperous, they still live as though they were nearly penniless. (See Luke 12:32.)

Poverty or riches is really an offspring of your thoughts.

God desires that His children be blessed so that they in turn can bless others. You're an instrument through which God's love, truth, beauty, and finances can flow. Think differently: "How can I bless and help others? What can I give?"

> ### *Your goals are only as worthy as the effort required to achieve them.*

The story is told of an eagle egg that fell out of the nest and rolled down a little hill into a prairie chicken nest. The prairie hen hatched this strange egg and accepted the chick as her own. When the chick grew up, he didn't know he was an eagle. He thought he was a prairie chicken.

When the eagle looked into the sky and saw the eagles flying, he probably thought, *I wonder what it would be like to be able to do that?* He could have, but he didn't know how to reach out and set a goal. He didn't even consider jumping out of a tree and trying to fly. He thought he was a prairie chicken, so he lived the prairie chicken life.

You may have hidden potential that will never be realized unless you allow your God-given dreams to rise to the surface and find expression in your plans and goals. You need to prepare now for what God is going to do in your future.

One of my good pastor friends, Peter Doseck, told me on the telephone one day, "You will never discover God in the capacity that you are about to discover Him without being where you are right now."

Think about that. You could be on the verge of a great adventure.

You say, "But I hate to speak before people. I get butterflies in my stomach." Just teach those butterflies to fly in formation.

"I want to speak to somebody about the Lord, but I'm shy." Then lead other shy people to the Lord.

You can be a success. You can make it happen.

Keep Your Target in Sight

Remember, you can't hit the target if you don't have one. That's why you need to know what your goals are. There are several ways to keep your target in focus.

1. Write your goals.

Because Satan wants to defeat you, he will try to diffuse your enthusiasm and undermine your goals. To counter his attacks, keep a record of your goals and successes. Write your goals down on paper. Know exactly what you want to accomplish. Don't just leave it to chance.

Only 5 percent of people have goals, and only 2 or 3 percent of them write them down. Writing your goals reinforces them in your own thinking and reminds you of your commitment.

My goals are written down where I can see them and pray about them — in my home, in my car, and in my briefcase all the time so I can constantly review them to see if I'm on track.

> ### Dreams fail without plans and goals.

2. Set deadlines.

When you write your goals, place deadlines on them.

When a couple plans to get married, they don't say, "We're getting married some day, some time."

Family and friends ask, "Well, when are you going to get married?"

"Oh, I don't know. We'll set a date sometime."

In 1960, John Kennedy said, "In ten years, we will put a man on the moon." He told the people around the table that day, "Write it down."

Some of those present didn't want to write it down. They thought it was crazy, but they did it. And in 1969, America put the first man on the moon.

Jim Agard said that it was no problem to put a man on the moon. It was just a challenge to get him there.

You can never accomplish more than you plan.

But you don't have to waste a lot of time trying to figure out what your goals should be. If you have a dream, you will know what steps to take to get there.

3. Develop a mental picture of your goal.

The Bible refers to mental visions 102 times.

Jesus used parables to paint pictures for us.

Your mind will develop mental pictures of what you think about. If I say I have a bear in my bathtub and her cubs are in the kitchen, you can see them in your mind. Suggestion is power.

If possible, get a photo that approximates your goal and put it where you see it every day. Television is powerful because you not only hear the message, you see the pictures. It puts a vivid image in your mind.

I have pictures of my goals. When I look at them, I pray, "Lord, I thank You for helping me reach this goal."

4. Develop a plan for reaching your goals.

In order to put together an intelligent plan for a project, you should first gather all the information needed to get where you want to go. Then acquire the necessary tools, training, experience, and materials to get there.

Sometimes the path from our dream to our goals needs to be divided into more manageable portions. When a project is gigantic, it can seem impossible. The drive from Seattle to Florida cannot be made in a single day, there must be rest stops along the way, where we can sleep and recharge, eat and refuel.

> *God will never give you a*
> *dream without giving you*
> *the ability and qualifications*
> *to accomplish that dream.*

He will also help you make plans to reach your goal. Then your dreams will fuel your fire so your plans can be well-laid and you can accomplish God's purpose.

When you are working on doing what God has called you to do and have set goals, your faith increases, making it possible for you to really believe you are going to reach them.

5. Water your goals with prayer.

After you've been specific with your goals, water them with prayer every day. Goals are like plants. Without daily attention and constant care, they will shrivel up and die.

6. Re-evaluate your goals periodically.

You need checkpoints on the way to reaching your goals. Check your progress to see how you are doing.

Your goals may expand to meet new challenges or be raised beyond your original expectations. Sometimes as you go along, your faith is encouraged, and you reach out further than you had anticipated. Successful experiences will teach you how to expand your goals.

Your goal is to win five people to the Lord this year, but you win four in January, so you say, "I can do this every month." You expand your vision, but you stick with the plan. That's vitally important.

You may be planning to buy a used car, but you find a new car that costs a little more money. You drive it, and then all of a sudden your goal has changed.

Be sensitive to change, and remember: You are either a thermostat or a thermometer. A thermometer reports outside conditions. That's all it does. But a thermostat can be adjusted to control the conditions.

You need to check your condition at certain points, and make adjustments as needed. That way you will be able to keep in total unity with God to reach your desired goal.

Your Goals for Your Future

This year:

1.

2.

3.

4.

Five years from now:

1.

2.

3.

4.

Ten years from now:

1.

2.

3.

4.

9

Achieving Your God-given Goals

I love people who set goals because they encourage me to reach beyond myself. When I discuss my goals with them, they understand and spur me on.

Let me give you a word of advice: Never discuss your goals with someone who has no goals. They will only try to discourage you and make you feel worthless, useless, and hopeless. It will certainly not help you.

All the winners I know set goals, and they inspire others to dream and plan. Their goals burn in their hearts.

I love speaking for my friend in Korea, Dr. David Yonggi Cho, who has the largest church congregation in the world. He started with the goal of reaching several hundred people for Christ. When he reached that goal, he decided he would set a bigger goal to reach a thousand. He did that. Then it grew to five thousand, then twenty thousand, then seventy thousand, then half a million.

Dr. Cho keeps reaching goals because he has faith that he will reach them. He has a plan, and he knows what his goal is. He keeps expanding and setting new goals.

> *Never discuss your goals with someone who has no goals.*

The Bible says that as a man thinks in his heart, so is he. If you think your goals can be reached, you will think and talk success. You'll talk prosperity. You'll talk growth. You'll talk victory.

Billy Graham has a goal. He has a dream and a plan. Oral Roberts, Casey Treat, Don Mears, Ron Stevens, Clyde Wasdin, Karl Strader, Bill Hybels, Tommy Barnett — we could go on and on and on — these are people who set goals. Because they set goals, they reap success.

Those who operate under God's laws of success learn how to develop their gifts and believe they will succeed. Because their dreams come from the heart of God, they submit to His requirements when they make their plans and set their goals.

What Does God Require?

To achieve your God-given goals, you must meet God's requirements for success. You can't just sit back and expect God to do all the work. Let's look at what you need to do to accomplish the goals you have set.

1. God's goals require sacrifice.

Even God has goals.

What is God's main goal? To prepare mankind for communion with Him forever because, in a sense, God is a little lonesome. He has angels, but they are not created in *His* image. They are beings created to serve Him. They are not free moral agents as we are. God wants communion with mankind. That is His ultimate goal.

His dream is to save mankind. His plan to accomplish that dream was to sacrifice Jesus, His Son, and the goal was to prepare us for eternal communion with Him for ever and ever.

Some dreams require sacrifice on our part.

> *Our motives are far more important than our dreams, plans, or goals.*

During the French Revolution, a young man named Charles Dornay had been condemned to die by the guillotine for a crime that he had committed. A young English lawyer, Sidney Carton, was determined to spare Dornay's life, not just for his sake but for the sake of Dornay's wife and child.

Carton managed to get into the dungeon on the night before the execution and change clothes with Dornay. The following day, Carton was executed as Charles Dornay.

Jesus said, "Greater love has no man than this, that a man lay down his life for his friends" (John 15:13).

As Christians, our goal should be to follow God's example of loving sacrifice. We may even be required to sacrifice our own goals to help others achieve theirs.

Large corporations often ask the question about their product, "Will it sell?" The question should be, "Will it serve?" If it serves, it will sell.

Some people make money their ultimate goal. Money in itself is not evil, but the love of money is. To say that money is evil is equivalent to saying that because one bank went under, all banks are bad. Or to saying that all churches are corrupt because there is a hypocrite in your church. Or to saying that marriage is wrong because some people get divorced.

Our motives are far more important than our dreams, plans, or goals. If our motives are impure or greedy, God cannot bless our plans and goals.

2. God's goals require obedience.

God doesn't do everything. He leaves some things up to us to do. He wants us to set goals.

The apostle Paul said, "I press toward the mark (the target)." Get lined up. Know where you're aiming. Shoot at the target.

The walls of Jericho fell after the Israelites marched around them in obedience to God. The people did their part, and then God caused the walls to collapse.

God had given Israel a dream: They would possess the land. The people were able to take over Canaan, not only because they had a dream, a plan, and a goal, but because they obeyed.

Naaman had a dream. He wanted to be healed of his leprosy. When the prophet told him to dip in the river, he obeyed — although reluctantly. He was healed because he did what he was supposed to do. He obeyed.

3. God's goals require courage.

Exodus chapters 7 through 10 tell how, through a series of plagues, signs, and miracles, Moses led God's chosen people out of Egypt. Although he left with six hundred thousand people, besides children, only two of the Israelites who left Egypt were able to complete the journey. From our standpoint, that's not a very good success rate.

The first group of Israelites who fled Egypt failed to reach their ultimate goal because of fear. Their spies came back and said the Promised Land was full of giants and warriors too fierce for them to defeat. Fear stopped them dead in their tracks, and God sent them back into the desert for the next forty years.

> ## Don't let fear stand in the way of fulfilling your dreams, plans, and goals.

Don't put up with fear in your life.

One day, as a young boy was coming home from school, he saw a bulldog barking. It scared him, so he went around the block the other way. After several days of this detour, he got tired of walking the extra distance and said, "I will go down that street. I'll get a stick and I'll hit that bulldog, and he'll know who is in charge!"

When he got close to the barking bulldog, he looked it straight in the face and began to laugh. Then he put down his stick. The bulldog didn't have any teeth.

Most of our fears are like toothless bulldogs. If we muster the courage to face them, we'll find they were harmless after all.

When God first called Moses in the desert where he had fled, Moses was afraid to return to Egypt. As a young man, Moses had killed an Egyptian, buried him in the sand, and got himself on the "ten most wanted list." After much persuasion, Moses finally found the courage to return to Egypt and fulfill God's plan for his life.

Don't let fear stand in the way of fulfilling your dreams, plans, and goals.

4. God's goals require faith.

You have the faith of God in you to create whatever it is you want to create. You can believe that victory is yours because Christ's victory is your victory. His triumph is your triumph.

Dr. Cho didn't begin with the goal of winning five hundred thousand people to Christ in six months. He had a smaller goal, and when that one was reached, he raised it, and raised it again and again.

Don't wait for things to be totally like you want them to be. Get out and do it. You can learn by trial and error. Believe that God honors faith, and that you can attain your goals.

> *Sometimes faith means risking what we value most to achieve what is most important to God.*

In the Book of Exodus, we read how God used a woman to set His plan in motion. You probably remember how Moses' mother hid him for three months because Pharaoh had decreed the killing of all Israelite baby boys. When Pharaoh's daughter came down to the river to bathe, she had her servants fetch the little boat carrying Moses and rescued him from the river. This heathen socialite didn't know God had a dream, plan, and goal for Moses to deliver Israel from bondage.

When the baby cried, it softened the heart of this pagan woman, and she wanted to find someone to take care of the child. Moses' big sister was waiting close by as her mother had directed her. She said, "I know someone who can take care of this baby," and she went to get her mother.

Moses' mother had a dream and a plan, and she took the necessary risks to achieve her desired goal.

Sometimes faith means risking what we value most to achieve what is most important to God.

5. God's goals require a positive attitude.

Get rid of your suspicion, resentment, self-pity, and other negative emotions that drain enthusiasm and energy. God will give you His peace (see Phil. 4:6-7).

Don't lay the blame for your situation on your mate, your mother-in-law, events, taxes, the government, the economy, or the world system. Don't be a victim of the circumstances. Instead of allowing yourself to be defeated, become the master of negative situations and turn them into positives.

When your thinking is in tune with God, your mind will have a new outlook and you'll begin to think differently about situations. You'll be an easier and happier person to live with and be around.

As a Christian, you are spiritually equipped to

overcome every challenge. Expect your life to have meaning and direction. You have to think right for things to happen.

You can believe that God will help you and see you through. There isn't anything that you cannot do.

6. God's goals require determination.

You need goals to give you a sense of purpose.

If you have no goals in life, you will drift along spiritually. You'll only go to church when you feel like it and stay home when you don't. You will give to God's work or serve Him if it's not too much out of your way. You will read the Bible only if you have time — which, of course seldom happens.

> *You can never accomplish*
> *more than you plan.*

One of my goals is to win people to Christ and get them involved in church. As I travel, speaking in some of the greatest churches in the world, I share seven ways to make faith pledges of new families to your church. We pledge finances, why can't we pledge families?

I have personally pledged to bring in a certain number of families each year to my home church. My pastor knows how many I've pledged and that, as I write this, I'm on schedule.

I have my own method of winning these families to the Lord and then getting them involved in our local church. Although the term "discipling" has been overworked and misused, it is still true that a new believer needs nurturing, fellowship, and an example. That's how I work with these people to help them become active members of our church.

I meet some who are newcomers to town and are already Christians but are looking for a church home. I have them check out our church. I introduce them to others in the church and do my best to help them get established. It works because I have a plan and specific goals.

If you are determined and stay on course, you'll meet your goals, too.

7. God's goals require prayer.

Because you have God-given goals, you can ask God to make you a success and to make you fruitful. You can cultivate those goals through prayer, but you need God's help to accomplish them.

Don't think, "I'm going to try to do it all by my human effort." No, you need God. The Bible states, "It is not by might, nor by power, but by the Spirit, says the Lord." We must depend upon God.

You should never attempt to achieve your goals in natural energy without God in your life. You must believe that God gives you victory and that He wants to see you through. He wants to help you reach your goals.

8. God's goals require patience and persistence.

God gave Moses a dream and a vision, but he had lessons to learn — some of them the hard way.

When the people murmured and complained for water, Moses struck the rock. But God had commanded him to *speak* to it. "Here, you rebels!" Moses screamed. This burst of rage cost him entrance into the Promised Land, in spite of his wonderful service.

Some of us are like Moses. If we aren't careful, we could miss the "Promised Land" because of anger and impatience.

> *Don't miss your "Promised Land" because of anger and impatience.*

Don't allow yourself to live in the past and wallow in the defeats that you experienced there. It is a complete waste of time and energy to relive things you no longer have the power to change. Learn from past errors, and don't repeat them.

When macadamia nut trees are cultivated, the first year the tree looks like it won't live; the second year it really looks terrible; and the third year it looks like it should be dug up and burned. The fourth and fifth years are not much better. But the sixth year, the tree begins bearing fruit, and it continues to bear fruit for up to one hundred years.

God doesn't want you to give up when things look bad and the going gets tough.

From Dreams to Fulfillment

God wants to help you bear fruit. He wants to help you achieve your goal. He wants you to exercise your faith. He wants you to get every answer you are praying for. He wants to put you on top of a mountain of answered prayer and reach an altitude of victory. There's nothing that can't be done.

Remember, winners set specific goals and write them down. Their goals are solid and serious and have deadlines. They have checkpoints for progress and are willing to take action and even risks if necessary.

You have dreams. Let your life move in the direction of those dreams. Raise the level of your faith expectations. Change your thinking. Choose to change your future now.

Keep your dreams general. Move into plans set by God, because if you don't plan, you won't succeed.

Very few people who reached their goals ever did so without effort, negative situations, and struggles. Whatever you are believing God for in your life — a successful marriage, a successful business, a successful personal life — whatever it is, believe from this day forward that your dreams will come true and that the future is bright for you.

Don't let anybody derail your thinking or destroy your dream. Don't give up. Let faith feed those dreams. You can change your world.

God has a plan for your life, and He wants you to reach your goals. Every dreamer has a vision —

without a dream, you will not make it. But you will make it because you do have a dream.

> ### *If you don't plan, you won't succeed.*

Believe and plan and work and expect that God will bring to pass what He wants to do in your life. The King of kings and the Lord of lords will see you through every challenge in your life.

Start believing and talking that way, and you will succeed. You have what it takes. God created you to be a winner. Your dreams can be exciting, your plans can be organized, and your God-given goals can be achieved.

1. Be unafraid.
2. Be aware of your mission.
3. Don't be confused by negative people or situations.
4. Be possessed by a unique sense of responsibility.
5. Dream
       Learn
            Believe
                 Plan
                      Work

And you will succeed.

Guidelines

1. After accepting Christ into your life, begin every day with God — praying and reading the Bible.

2. Attend a Bible-believing church faithfully.

3. Tithe 10 percent of your total income to your church.

4. Read only positive books and listen to positive tapes.

5. Be a positive force in a negative world daily.

6. Develop a good attitude. Remember life is 10 percent what happens to you and 90 percent how you react.

7. Never panic, give up, or get discouraged. Say, "God will help me handle whatever situation comes my way. I have dreams, plans, and goals."

8. Thank God daily for miracles.

9. Expect answers to every challenge.

Notes

Chapter 1

[1]Dave Williams, *Define Your Dreams* (Lansing, MI: Mount Hope Books, 1987).

Chapter 2

[1]Dexter Yager, *Don't Let Anybody Steal Your Dreams* (Springfield, MO: Restoration, 1978).

Chapter 7

[1]John Drescher, "A Parable of Fishless Fishermen," *Message of the Open Bible* (May, 1992).